An
Educated
Choice

An Educated Choice

Advice for Parents
of College-Bound Students

Frank A. Brock

P.O. BOX 817 • PHILLIPSBURG • NEW JERSEY 08865-0817

Library of Congress Control Number: 2006933167

All who have meditated on the art of governing mankind have been convinced that the fates of empires depends on the education of youth.

Aristotle

Contents

Acknowledgments

For sixteen years I had the great blessing of working at Covenant College, where I learned so much from my colleagues and from the college students. I also had the privilege of traveling extensively both within the United States and abroad, meeting thousands of parents, prospective students, and alumni as well as educators at other colleges. I have learned so much from so many.

The faculty, staff, and board of Covenant College not only deeply care about young people, but they are also extraordinarily competent. I greatly admire their knowledge and ability. A core conviction that we jointly hold is that each individual needs to first be transformed by the grace of God to the knowledge of God and then by grace to obedience to God. God wants us to work as redeemed human beings within the culture to transform fallen structures—families, churches, businesses, governments—in a way that reflects an answer to the Lord's Prayer: "Your kingdom come, your will be done on earth as it is in heaven" (Matt. 6:10). It is this culture of Covenant College that has prompted me to write this book, with the aspiration of helping improve higher education. If more parents seek a better education for their children, perhaps these children will better serve the world. I am deeply indebted to all those whom Covenant College represents—donors (especially the Maclellan Foundation), trustees, teachers, staff members, students, pastors, churches, and alumni.

I want to thank my wife, who has put up with this time-consuming project for five years and has encouraged me to stick with it. Finally, I want to thank my children and their spouses, all of whom have had at least part of their college education at Covenant College. All were tremendously shaped by Covenant and continue to support me and the college in ways that endear a father's heart.

Introduction

This book is written primarily for parents and educators of high school students who are college bound.

From 1987 until 2002 I was president of a four-year, residential college, and I have lived in a world of perpetual youth; the students' ages never change. I appreciate college students' openness and readiness to grow and learn. I love seeing students debate issues and get excited about an area of study. I enjoy the out-of-classroom aspects of college—students learning to be on their own, having fun, building lifelong friendships, maybe even finding their mate. I particularly enjoy getting students to see a bigger picture, to rise to the challenge of making an impact in a needy world. Many want to devote themselves to solving some of the world's problems, and I find that very encouraging.

As a college president, I have talked with thousands of students over those sixteen years. I am convinced that the college years are critical years when many crucial decisions are made—what career to pursue, whom to marry (or whether to marry at all or just live with someone), and where to live, to name just a few. They are years when students develop lifelong skills, such as learning to think, to communicate, and to relate. Important perspectives often emerge—a healthy or poor self-image, idealism or cynicism, concern for others or preoccupation with self, avoidance or acceptance of responsibility for personal actions. In college, students can meet the greatest minds of all time and learn from them. It is a time to see one's self in the larger context of history, of ideas, of culture, all of which have impacted each of us in various ways. It is a time of great energy and reflection.

However, most students barely comprehend the once-in-a-lifetime potential for learning and growth that the college experience provides. The adage "education is wasted on the young" is not really true, but it seems that way to the student who has difficulty understanding why what he or she is studying is important. Furthermore, students often do not realize how much the college experience varies from campus to campus. Consequently, many students—and their parents—do not realize how important it is to choose a good college.

There is no excuse for poor education, but I think good education begins with high expectations on the part of schools and families. Too many Americans have given in to mediocrity. One reason for this is that even parents don't know what to look for. Furthermore, many parents do not realize just how influential they can be in guiding their college-bound children in this process. High school students have a way of letting their parents know that their advice is not particularly wanted when, in truth, they want and need parental guidance. Going to college is not like going into the thirteenth grade.

Getting students involved in choosing a college is critical because it helps set the stage for learning. When parents ensure that students are involved in the process of choosing a college, students are far more likely to receive the benefits of a good education. Getting a degree is not the same as getting a good education. My investigations and experience suggest that the most important determinant of whether a student gets a good education is the student's own attitude (followed by the attitudes of their friends and the "learning environment" of the college). Just because a college happens to be close to home or cheap or where their friends go is no reason to choose a college, yet many students give these as the principal reasons for their choice.

If you want to know the types of things students look for in a college, look at the web site of the College Board (http://www.collegeboard.com). For the thousands of colleges listed, students are given the following types of information: the community where the college is located, the type of students attracted, the faculty, strong departments, housing, dining, recreation and activities, availability of services, and special programs. While I do not deny that these items have impact on the college experience, none really deals with what students are learning.

No matter what types of students it admits, a college, a good college, helps those students make significant progress in developing skills, knowledge, and values that will provide a foundation for the rest of life. (Just because a college admits above-average students does not mean it is a "good college"; the real question is how much a college helps its "above-average" students grow and develop.) In other words, a good college is a college that moves a student from one level to another, not just a college that gets good students and graduates good students who have not grown significantly.

The adage, "buyer beware," applies to college. The uncaring or unsuspecting student who fails to get a good education may never know it and may never recover. On the other hand, the student who develops a sound foundation may never give credit to his or her college preparation but will benefit from that foundation for the rest of his or her life.

This book seeks to go beyond the typical college guide to the heart of the issue: How do you ensure that students get a good education? First let's look at some basic assumptions.

- A good education makes a big difference in a person's life.
- Education is all about teachers and students. Everything else is fluff.
- Teachers matter.
- The curriculum matters.
- The educational community matters.
- A good education lasts a lifetime.
- Well-educated citizens benefit those around them.

Part of the difficulty of addressing what makes a good education is that students are not alike. Each student has his or her own history in terms of learning, personality, and motivation. Throughout the book, I have included illustrations from students I have known over the years. Part of the difficult task of parents and educators is to help each student realize his or her God-given potential. Even brothers and sisters are so different from each other that what works with one child may not work with another. Parents and educators need to help each student discern the type of educational environment that would best support him or her. I hope to help you as a parent understand something of the educational landscape and see that there are many types of learning communities with differing philosophies of education, all of which have different outcomes.

But how do you know what to look for? There is so much written about colleges that most parents throw up their hands, often opting for an easy, comfortable choice—an inexpensive, local college—rather than taking the time to search for a school where their child would flourish. In some ways, prospective users of higher education cannot see the forest for the trees.

But I will try to appeal to your common sense based on our common experience with life. By focusing on typical students, I hope to bring some of the larger philosophical issues concerning education closer to home to help you realize that real people are affected in significant ways by what goes on at college. I would add that college students are not only real people, they are important people. In just a few years, they will be running our businesses, providing for our health and education, and leading our government. They will be writers and artists who portray our culture and our future. They will be providing for us in our declining years. We dare not let them down by failing to give them a good education, or we will condemn subsequent generations, our grandchildren and great-grandchildren, to the damaging effects of ignorance, injustice, lack of economic opportunity, crime, and violence.

I admit the idealism of this book. But those of us in higher education need discerning customers. The only alternative to wiser and more discerning users of higher education is to have those in the educational establishment make your choices for you. And with more than 2,100 four-year, nonprofit[1] colleges, it is all too easy for educators to succumb to market pressures, to try to make students satisfied customers rather than give them an outstanding education.

If consumers can learn to make wise choices when it comes to health care, computers, houses, life insurance, etc., then surely families can learn to make wise choices when it comes to a college education. If this is not the case, then our society truly is in decline, and nothing other than a change in what we value can stop that decline. Choosing a college should force a person to think about what is important and to make a complex value judgment, one that has significant impact on his or her family's present and future financial situation. A good college-decision-making process is often several years long and requires research as well as frequent interaction between adults and young people.

I believe that college students are important and so is what they learn. I hope to help you think about what is important to you and your child. I hope that as we explore what happens when a student goes to college, you'll agree with Aristotle: "The future of the republic depends on the training of our youth."

1

What Do You Want from Your Child's Education?

The search for a college starts with the question, "What's important to you?" Let me give you some examples to illustrate how the answer to this question varies from person to person.

> Mary isn't sure what she wants to study. She's a good kid and always does what is expected, but she just hasn't focused on a career yet. The main question is, "What will Mary do if she is an English major and can't get a job when she gets out of college?"
>
> Jason is relational. He just hasn't grown up yet. He does okay in school, but his family isn't sure if he's ready to go off to college. Maybe he should just stay at home for a year and go to the community col-

lege. The main question is, "What happens if Jason goes off to college and flunks out?"

Allison is premed. She's wanted to be a doctor since she was a child, but she knows that getting into medical school is difficult. The main question is, "What's the medical school acceptance rate?"

Tom's father played baseball and Tom has been throwing a ball since he learned to walk. He's good enough to play Division One—at least that's what his parents think. The main question is, "How big is the scholarship and how strong is the baseball program?"

Ashley is shy. She would get lost in a big school and needs to be close to home. Her father says, "Ashley and her mother are very close. We want Ashley to be able to come home on weekends." The main question is, "Will there be a warm, nurturing environment that is close to home?"

Matt's father is a teacher. "We earn too much money to get financial aid and not enough to pay for an expensive college." Matt is taking all AP courses. The main question is, "Will you accept AP credit and what academic scholarships are available?"

Susie is more interested in boys than in college. She really doesn't want to sit down with her parents and talk about school. Her attitude is, "Don't worry. It will all work out. I can always get in at the last minute." The main question is, "When all of Susie's friends are accepted into college, will it be too late for Susie to apply and get into a good college?"

In spite of the different ways students approach the college decision, most feel intense pressure to go to college. Whether they admit it or not, all college-bound students know that "You can't get a good job without a college degree." Many believe that college degrees are so common that what really matters is getting into grad school. They feel the pressure to do well in high school so they can get into college.

And it's not just students who feel the pressure. Parents struggling to make ends meet know that life is tough and competitive, and they want their kids to have the best chance possible to succeed. There is an implicit assumption that virtually all parents seem to make: Going to college equals making more money. And no one wants their children to be poor—especially if the kids end up back home living with Mom and Dad. Too little thought is given to the question, "Is there a difference between getting a degree and getting a good education?"

The fact is that college graduates will have many different kinds of jobs paying a wide range of salaries. Most college graduates will end up making average salaries— yes, higher salaries than what those with just a high school degree will make, but nonetheless, just average salaries. It's the old Lake Wobegon story, in which all the parents think their kids are above average. Of course, it's great to have high aspirations for your children, but I am simply trying to be realistic. If you choose a college because you think it's going to ensure your child a good job, you are probably making the decision based on a false expectation. You might be setting up yourself and your child for disappointment.

Considering the emotional aspects of choosing a college is important. The prospect of going to college raises a series of complex emotions that vary as much in parents as in their children. Some parents vicariously live their lives through their children, and getting the child into a "good" college is important for the parents' ego. Some parents didn't go to or finish college, and they want to make sure their kids do better than they did. Some parents are strictly hands-off. They want their children to make the decision. Some parents are very controlling; *they* will decide which college their child attends. Some parents want their children close to home; other parents think it is important to get away from home. In some ways, the college choice seems to represent the deepest fears and aspirations that parents have for themselves and their children. From my experience in dealing with parents, there are several emotional "filters" through which parents seem to process information.

The first filter is financial. Parents don't want to embarrass their children or themselves by encouraging attendance at an expensive school they can't afford. Even though the national average family income of students who go to private colleges is about the same as the average family income of students who go to public universities, most families assume that a private college is out of the question. With an average U.S. family income of $46,737,[1] most families assume that their sons and daughters will have no option but to go to a state school. They've heard other parents talk about how expensive college is. Many parents are scared to talk to their children about a private education because they don't want to raise false hopes and they don't want their children to come out of college with large loans to pay off. Children pick up on their parents' concerns, and many conscientious students will say that they want to go to a public college just to avoid putting the family under any additional stress. I will devote an entire chapter to financial matters later in the book, but my conviction is that nothing is more expensive than a failed college experience and nothing is more valuable than a good education.

A second filter is location. More than half of all students attend a college or university within one hundred miles of home. This is a relatively new phenomenon that probably has more to do with the proliferation of higher-education institutions and their accessibility

20

than with finding a good fit. After all, we don't have to travel far to find a good restaurant, a good mall, a good theater, a good car, or a good house. Why should we have to travel far to find a good school? Choosing a college close to home may not only be perceived as convenient, it may also be perceived as less expensive, especially when you consider the cost of an automobile or airfare.

However, in a world of diverse people who have to learn to live together, we should be warring against provincialism. We should want students to leave old high school friends and meet new people. We should want them to go off to college and begin to experience living independently from their parents' care. And, most of all, we should recognize that finding a good fit between the student and the institution is far more important than convenience or cost. Even though there may be many institutions within two hundred miles of home, this does not mean any of them would be best for a particular student.

A third filter is familiarity. Often the reason given for choosing a particular college is the parents' personal acquaintance with students who have gone to the school and who seem to like it. Perhaps this is the most disturbing reason of all. For most of us college was a wonderful stage of life, and we have many pleasant memories of our experience. To be honest, it really isn't that hard to find a college that a student will enjoy. In almost any college, a person will find a group of friends with comparable interests, plenty of things to do, and lots of time to do them. Whether the college has five hundred students or fifty thousand students, each student usually has a group of friends that numbers closer to ten or twenty people than any larger number. Almost every college has so many activities that a student could never do them all. Few colleges require so much homework that there is no time for anything else. But it's not un-common for a student to tell you how much he or she enjoys college and then to drop out at the end of the semester. So parents need to be wary when students they know seem to be enjoying their college. Choosing a col-lege merely because other students seem to be "enjoy-ing" the college does not mean your son or daughter will find a good education there.

The fourth filter is who makes the decision. I have sat with parents who have grilled me for an hour about every aspect of college life. They are often suspicious of every claim the college makes. They have read horror stories of the ways colleges use figures to paint the most favorable picture of the school. They want to see the col-lege crime report; they want to know the school's reten-tion; they want to know how many adjuncts the school uses. On the other hand, I have met parents who told their children as early as the seventh grade that it was up to them whether they would even go to college. Some parents take their children on college campus tours. Some parents send their children to visit colleges. Some students go to college having never seen the campus and without knowing a single student.

It is important to talk with your child about his or her degree of involvement. Do this, recognizing that the typ-ical high school experience is quite limited. When I took my oldest to visit his first college, the biggest surprise for him was the size differential. Even though he at-tended a high school with an impressive physical plant and lived in a town with several colleges, my son had no idea that a college campus could occupy forty acres of land and take at least ten minutes to walk from one end to another. He did not know that in college you might have to walk from one building to another in between classes and that you might do so without seeing anyone you recognize. Most high school students do not fully understand the radical difference that exists between high school and college.

Therefore, I have come to believe that parents need to be aware of the filters they use in looking at colleges and to self-consciously determine what really is important and why. I'm convinced that young students desire more and more a meaningful relationship and dialogue with one or more adults. But although they desire this, often they do not know how to start a dialogue or form a relationship that requires a significant amount of trust and mutual respect, a more mature relationship, not just one between a parent and child. So it is important for you to initiate the dialogue and to talk about the decision-making process. Students need to know what to expect in terms of help and guidance (whether wanted or not). I am convinced that a good process will result in creating an *intentional* student, one who knows where he or she is going and why. Such intentionality will greatly increase the student's own desire to make the most of the college experience, thus significantly increasing the likelihood of getting a good education.

Some parents have said to me that the college choice is the most important decision a person will ever make. They argue that it is in college that a person decides what to do, whom to marry, where to live, and what the yardstick for success is. There is no doubt that the college years are important years. Sadly, many students who enter college never graduate, and many others who do gain a diploma fail to get a good education.

I'm a believer in the 80/20 rule. This rule says that most things seem to divide out along the lines of 80 percent and 20 percent. (For example, 20 percent of the stores have 80 percent of the customers.) Perhaps the most important point that I can make is the obvious one: A student can get a good education at almost any school, but not every school gives a good education.

Look for a good school. I would suggest that 80 percent of the students who receive a good education get that education in one of the 20 percent of colleges that consistently serve students by providing a good education. And the colleges that consistently provide a good education are not always "high-profile" colleges that are inaccessible to the average family. To the contrary, there are many excellent colleges, both private and public, providing a wide variety of programs in a wide variety of settings that would benefit a wide variety of students. What is important is to know what's important in helping a young person look for a college.

2

College Education Today

So how do you negotiate the ocean of higher education? With more than 2,100 four-year, nonprofit colleges and universities, how do you know where to start? It always helps to know history, so let's examine how higher education evolved to the present state.

Higher Education in America

The idea of formal college-level education is a relatively new idea. Prior to the twentieth century high school was the end of formal education for most people. Those who went on to college usually attended a college of less than one thousand students to pursue further studies in theology, law, or medicine. "When the twentieth century dawned, only 4 percent of Americans between the ages of 18 and 21 attended college or university."[1]

The development of universities as research centers became commonly accepted. With research came an explosion of knowledge, and with that explosion came a revolution in higher education. Professors in philosophy, religion, and the humanities began to be replaced by scholars who began to apply a "scientific method" to the study of the world.

This scientific method, accepted as the norm today, used objective evidence to see how things actually worked. Instead of simply accepting such things as sickness, lightning, and economic cycles, scholars began to study them to see how and why they occurred. The physical sciences pushed back the frontiers, and new discoveries became common. (Remember, the automobile, telephone, and electricity are inventions or discoveries that only became common in the twentieth century.) The scientific method was also used to study the mind, human relations, government, and work, with the result of entirely new disciplines of scientific inquiry, such as psychology, sociology, political science, and economics. Even religion, especially the origin of the Bible, became an object of the scientific approach. The scientific methodology and the scholars who employed this methodology developed important insights that helped unlock mysteries that had baffled the sages for centuries. The number of academic disciplines exploded, and more and more students began going to college to pursue a variety of careers.

Following World War II, higher education exploded and became a "growth industry." The GI Bill of Rights included the right to receive a college education. From the perspective of government leaders, the association between economic development and education was firmly established. From the perspective of thousands of individuals desiring to enter the workforce, the association between education and personal career advancement was also firmly established. "Today, more than 80 percent of high school students aspire to higher education, and well over 70 percent actually enroll in some form of post-secondary education within two years of high school graduation."[2] This is a dramatic change that has occurred in only one hundred years.

The inherent value of education became so evident that no reasonable person could argue against it. While elementary and secondary schools served local communities, colleges and universities tended to serve statewide, even national communities. State political leaders found that one of the easiest ways to raise taxes is to improve educational opportunity, so large, low-tuition state universities became very common. Education had always been expensive, and funding it had never been easy, so the entry of the state was welcome relief to many beleaguered educators. (The history of private colleges was marked by periods of extreme financial exigency.) With public funding came more financial stability and far greater resources than were ever available to private institutions.

What was driving higher education was an economic demand of hitherto unknown proportions for more college-educated students. This demand translated into statewide systems of higher education, with boards of regents whose primary job was to provide the universities with the resources needed. Everyone assumed that the faculty members, under the direction of academic administrators, would intelligently prioritize how resources would be utilized.

Recent Trends

However, a subtle and unforeseen change was occurring in higher education. These trends were at work when parents of today's students were in college but have continued at an accelerated pace. Consider the 1982 summary of these changes as described by the Association of American Colleges:

> For the first two hundred years of American higher education the course of study was shaped by the authority of tradition, seldom challenged and easily accommodating both new learning and changing social conditions. The degree—there was only one, the B.A.—was a passport to the learned professions; most of the nation's work was happily and effectively done by people who had not gone to college. The American college at first was essentially a determined provincial echo of an English college.
>
> The authority of tradition was undermined in the nineteenth century, particularly after the Civil War, by the emerging professional academicians. Holders of the Ph.D. degree, they were trained to be responsible to a particular body of knowledge, a discipline (English, history, biology) and to a style of learning that, although particular to that discipline, was shaped by the methods of investigation, concepts, and empirical values of science. The impact of their growing authority on the traditional course of study was immense: not only did many new disciplines and subjects find their way into the course of study but the concept of a wholly elective curriculum was advanced as an instrument for facilitating study of the new subjects. Faculty control over the curriculum became lodged in departments that developed into adept protectors and advocates of their own interests, at the expense of institutional responsibility and curricular coherence.
>
> At the same time a dynamic and increasingly industrial society created new demands for technical skills, demands that were translated into formal bodies of knowledge that emerged in hundreds of new degree programs that challenged the supremacy of the B.A. degree, whatever its changing content. The emergence of the

American university in the late nineteenth century—the result of the coming together of the English college tradition, the research ideal of the German university, and the American ideal of the university as an instrument of public service—bombarded the old curriculum with an explosion of new subjects, courses, programs, and degrees. The American university developed into a magnificent democratic institution. Its libraries, laboratories, and scholars' studies became busy centers of inquiry, producing significant new knowledge at an accelerating rate. But dismay with the incoherence and lack of cohesion that resulted led in the early decades of this century to various devices to stem the tide of disarray: concentration and distribution, general education requirements, comprehensive examinations. By the time of World War II, tradition, the professional academicians, and society itself shared authority over what was going on in our colleges and universities.

Since World War II, American higher education has experienced a prolonged surge of growth. Colleges and universities more than doubled in number and many, especially public institutions, grew prodigiously. Enrollments in degree credit courses more than quadrupled. Bachelor's degrees more than trebled.[3]

Let us examine the dimensions of this enrollment growth by first looking at the percentage of high school graduates enrolled in college for the years following 1960.

Year	%
1960	45.1
1965	50.9
1970	51.8
1975	50.7
1980	49.3
1985	57.7
1990	59.9
1995	61.9
1998	65.6

Data from U.S. Census Bureau, "Statistical Abstract of the U.S.: 2000," 182.

29

Along with a larger percentage of students going from high school to college came adult education. More and more adults, often called nontraditional students, began to take college-level courses. Many of these students enrolled in community colleges. Many others enrolled in evening or weekend courses as part-time students. In 1960 there were only 451,000 students enrolled in two-year colleges; by 1997, this number had increased more than tenfold to 5,606,000.[4] By fall of 2000 only 71 percent of the 21,401,000 students enrolled as undergraduates were full-time students, and 31 percent of the full-time students were 22 years old or older.[5]

The combination of more high school graduates going to college, more adult students returning to college, and more part-time students led to dramatic increases in total enrollment. Following is a graph and table showing enrollment growth that has occurred since 1950.[6] The chart shows enrollment in private colleges is 2.8 times greater than in 1950, while enrollment in public colleges is 9.7 times greater than in 1950.

With growth in the total number of students enrolled in public universities came the phenomenon of the large

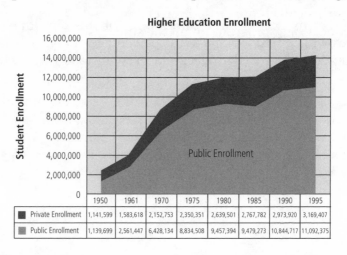

Higher Education Enrollment

	1950	1961	1970	1975	1980	1985	1990	1995
Private Enrollment	1,141,599	1,583,618	2,152,753	2,350,351	2,639,501	2,767,782	2,973,920	3,169,407
Public Enrollment	1,139,699	2,561,447	6,428,134	8,834,508	9,457,394	9,479,273	10,844,717	11,092,375

school. The size range varies significantly depending on whether the school is a public or private institution. The average public college has almost ten thousand students, while the average private college has less than eighteen hundred students.

While 85 percent of all private colleges have less than 2,500 students, 68 percent of all public institutions have more than 2,499 students.

Enrollment	Public	Private
Less than 1,000 students	194	1,366
1,000 to 2,499 students	356	538
2,500 to 4,999 students	386	190
More than 5,000 students	721	134
Total	1,657	2,228

Data from *The Chronicle of Higher Education, Almanac Issue* (31 August 2001): 20.

Many Americans seem to think that bigger means better, and this book would be of little interest if, in fact, larger universities meant better universities. Undoubtedly, a university of ten thousand students can offer more programs, more library resources, and more facilities. However, breadth of programs does not necessarily translate into quality programs; on the contrary, it is intrinsically more difficult to create a cohesive, quality educational program for all the students.

The Association of American Colleges report asserts that there was an unintended consequence of all this growth: "The accelerating democratization of higher education—the opening of access, the tremendous numbers—has created in students a new and commanding authority over the course of study. The interests of students demonstrated by their selection of courses have increasingly helped to shape what has been taught, why and how."[7]

It would appear that as colleges grow larger, there is less and less coherence in the curriculum. This is due to several factors. First, a large enrollment of students requires a large faculty. With a student/faculty ratio of 17 to 1, a college of 1,700 would have 100 faculty members, but a college of 10,000 would have almost 588 faculty members.

With one hundred faculty members, it is possible to have the entire faculty meet in a single room to discuss the things that all students need to know. The number of students is not that large, and there are not that many programs.

When there are hundreds of faculty members, the faculty typically elects delegates so that a delegated faculty makes decisions. These delegates come from programs that are far more diverse. With many more disciplines represented, it is far more difficult to reach agreement simply because there is more "diversity" and less "unity" among those who compose the *"uni-versity."*

A second consequence of larger schools is a much more complex task of administration for presidents and deans who must manage such institutions. The tasks of developing new programs, designing a campus, raising money, and so forth are so demanding that little leadership can be given to making the program more coherent. Often the administrators are trying to arbitrate between competing departments rather than managing the institution as a whole. Universities have become more like business conglomerates with many separate and independent departments.

Finally, with larger schools comes a more market-driven orientation. As quoted previously, "The interests of students demonstrated by their selection of courses have increasingly helped to shape what has been taught, why and how. What is now going on is almost anything, and it goes on in the name of the bachelor's degree."[8]

The development of large public universities was aided by a dramatic shift in the admissions process. In

1950 a person felt fortunate to get into college and to be able to afford it. But now nearly every student who wants to go to college can find a college that he or she can afford and that will accept him or her. Most high school students make A's and B's, and that is all most colleges require. Students do not even have to do a lot of homework to make those grades; surveys show that college-bound students say they had very little homework in high school. Students used to worry about getting into college; today enrollment-driven colleges worry about getting students. Public universities receive state appropriations based on enrollment, and tuition is the largest source of revenue for virtually all of the private colleges.

In summary, public colleges tend to offer students a variety of courses. If there are required courses, they are typically "distribution" requirements, meaning that the student can select from a variety of courses. For example, a student may have a distribution requirement of a lab science course, but the student can choose from a large number of courses in fields as diverse as physics or psychology. Similarly, a student may select from literally hundreds of courses in the area of the humanities; seldom is a student required to take a single course, such as American history. Students have become consumers, deciding what courses they will take. Colleges have become like malls, trying to offer what students want.

Student demand drives the number of degrees earned. Consider the top ten categories of degrees earned (a total of 1,184,406 bachelor's degrees).

Top Ten Degrees Earned in 1997–1998

Types of Bachelor's Degrees	%
1 Business and Management	19
2 Social Sciences	11

Types of Bachelor's Degrees	%
3 Education	9
4 Health Professions	7
5 Psychology	6
6 Biology/Life Sciences	6
7 Engineering	5
8 Visual and Performing Arts	4
9 Communications	4
10 English Language	4
Total	75

Data from *The Chronicle of Higher Education, Almanac Issue* (31 August 2001): 25.

Many people associate a liberal arts education with a college education. However, the term "liberal arts" has traditionally stood for courses in subjects in the humanities (English, history, philosophy, religion, etc.), the arts (art and music), the social sciences (political science, psychology, sociology, economics, etc.), and the natural sciences (chemistry, biology, botany, physics, etc.). Professional degrees are more vocationally oriented and include degrees in business, education, health professions, engineering, and communications. By 1986, only one in four bachelor's degrees was awarded in the liberal arts.[9]

Further evidence of the loss of coherence in educational institutions is the decline of core courses. When colleges were small and there were few majors, most graduates took the exact same curriculum. But as colleges grew in enrollment and in the number of majors, colleges tried to decide what the common learning experience should be. Such core requirements stipulated, for example, that all students should take English composition, American literature, Western civilization, college algebra, physical education, speech, a foreign language, etc. *Core* courses are those courses that each student takes, such as English composition, and *distribution* requirements are those courses that allow some choice, such as taking a foreign language (without specifying which language). Both *core* courses and *distribution* courses are part of the *core requirement* for graduation.

In 1964, colleges required an average of 6.9 mandatory courses; by 1993 this number dropped to 2.5 mandatory courses.[10] The National Association of Scholars concludes:

> The prevailing unwillingness to see priorities within general education programs, together with the growing disinclination to insist on rigorous standards for completing them, suggests that undergraduate education has been substantially undervalued as an institutional objective. It also suggests that most institutions are no longer seriously committed to ensuring that their students are exposed to broad surveys of basic subject matter. . . . The large majority have chosen instead to disguise virtually unrestricted options behind a facade of structure afforded by what are now generally called "distribution requirements."[11]

Research Universities

No review of higher educational trends could ignore the role of research universities. With the rapid growth in higher education came a demand for many more faculty members, and most of these faculty members came from research universities.

The general public does not fully understand the term "research university." The names of the research universities are among the most well-known schools, Johns Hopkins, University of Michigan, Massachusetts Institute of Technology, Cornell University, and Harvard, to name a few. These institutions do at least two things that distinguish them from other colleges and universities: They hire faculty whose primary job is research, and they have large graduate programs that grant Ph.D.

degrees. These Ph.D.s become the faculty at most other colleges.

Research is big business. Each year *The Chronicle of Higher Education* lists the top institutions in total research and development spending. In 2000, 56 institutions were listed, and the amount of money varied from a low of $140,589,000 (University of Texas Southwestern Medical Center at Dallas) to a high of $829,241,000 (Johns Hopkins). The amount of money spent on research at such institutions is far larger than the entire budget of many nonresearch universities. Since most research occurs at the graduate level and not at the undergraduate level, the impact of research on undergraduate education varies considerably and is the subject of debate.

Similarly, the teaching of graduate students has a mixed result for undergraduates. Some professors teach both graduates and undergraduates, but at a research university there is often more prestige associated with teaching graduate students than undergraduate students. Less contact with students is associated with teaching graduate students; there are fewer of them, and they are not so hard to motivate. Finally, pay scales at research universities are considerably higher than at teaching colleges. Consequently, it is difficult to get the best professors to teach undergraduates.[12]

Colleges seeking new faculty desire, and usually require, a Ph.D. One should not forget that a Ph.D. is a research degree. Earning a Ph.D. requires doing original research and writing and defending a thesis. Therefore, most college professors, even those not at research universities, are trained as scholars and not as teachers. A teacher is someone whose great skill is making complex subject matter intelligible and relevant. A scholar is not necessarily a teacher. Individuals who are pursuing a Ph.D. are often used by the university to teach, and their title is "graduate assistant." In this capacity, they get practical experience teaching, but they are not taught to teach. Only elementary, middle, and high school teachers are actually trained as "teachers."

While president of a college that has a teaching faculty, I often interviewed prospective professors. One of the questions I ask is whether the professor loves the discipline or loves to see students learn. Sometimes I could almost see the applicant squirm. For many faculty members, to join a teaching college is tantamount to ending their career. In recent years, there has been an attempt to emphasize the scholarship of teaching and to promote faculty members who excel as teachers and not just as researchers. It is difficult to ascertain the success of such programs.

The impact of the research university on modern education is enormous. Some would go so far as to say that the research university is the foundation of a modern industrial economy.[13] Countries around the world have copied the American model, and it exists in almost all the developed countries in some form or another. Research is critically important; no one would deny that. But for many schools, the unintended result of the pursuit of new knowledge has been a decline in the importance of teaching undergraduate students.

My main point is that the typical faculty member is a scholar first and a teacher second. In many universities, it is impossible to advance without doing research. Even where this is not the case, the type of person who becomes a professor is the type of person attracted by a research university with large, well-funded programs. People trained in research do not necessarily think about educating the whole person; they tend to think more about teaching another person about their own area of scholarly interest.

Conclusion

People tend to think that educators are shaping what college students are learning. I am convinced that this is not the case. Students' perception of the job market is determining what students major in, but this does not really tell what students are learning. Academic departments are, for the most part, independent of the college administration. In most colleges, especially the large ones, there is not a core curriculum, so students, even students who go to the same university but major in different subjects, are essentially deciding what they will learn.

In the first chapter, I tried to introduce the idea of the importance of seeking a good education. In this chapter, I hope that I have shown that this term means different things to different people. A good liberal arts education is different from a good professional education; a good research university has different aims than a good college focusing on undergraduate education. What is represented by a "college degree" varies widely and depends on both the type of degree and the quality of education provided. Consensus on what constitutes a good education is almost nonexistent, even among university faculty. Even consensus on what makes good teachers is not universal. In pursuit of what is good for the nation, especially the economy of the nation, higher education, especially research universities, is tempted to neglect the needs of undergraduate students for the needs of graduate students and research.

Before looking for a good education for a particular student, you need to help the student understand the vast differences between colleges and the expectation that each student will choose a curriculum that will meet his or her personal objectives for education.

3

Understanding Teens

Part of the challenge of writing on this subject is that students and families are so different from one another. It is difficult to be specific enough to be helpful and general enough to be applicable to the reader. However, I have spent a substantial portion of my time over the past sixteen years talking to students, and some general impressions began to emerge. I have also spoken with admissions personnel at Covenant College to check my observations against their impressions.

No two students are alike. Some come to college confidently; some come apprehensively. Some are far better prepared for college work than others. Some are mature and self-disciplined; some have almost no self-discipline. But nearly all students, even those from relatively poor families, are accustomed to material comforts. Their rooms are full of electronic gadgets, and they all seem to have a full wardrobe of clothes. In some ways students are all the same.

However, in ways that they are unaware of, students are different from the students of their parents' generation. Most students who enter college in 2002 were born in 1984. Let's assume their parents finished college in 1977 or thereabouts and started having children seven years later. Students entering college in 2002

> have no recollection of the Berlin Wall (it fell in 1989)
>
> cannot recall Ronald Reagan being president
>
> have never known tape players without CD players
>
> all have Internet access
>
> have always known cable TV
>
> see *Star Wars* as an old space movie done before they were born
>
> have seen during their teen years the greatest growth of the stock market in history
>
> are seeing for the first time in their lives an economic recession marked by rising unemployment
>
> have seen people having sex on their computer or television
>
> have always seen songs acted out on MTV

So what are the dominant cultural influences on today's students?

Prosperity, Inexperience, and Lack of Adult Contact

Students are completely unaware of how unusual they are in relation to the rest of the world. I took a group of students to Honduras to bring water to a village of fifty-seven homes without electricity or water. We dug a ditch two miles long, eighteen inches deep, and up a rocky mountain. Though such hard physical labor is common for most people in most countries, none of the students had ever worked so hard physically. We ate mostly tortillas and beans; the students had no idea that most people in the world consider a normal American breakfast of fresh fruit, cold milk, and packaged cereal to be a sumptuous meal, unavailable except to the very wealthy. The students had no idea that thousands die daily because they do not have clean water. The students had no idea that walking into a Wal-Mart, picking what you want off of a shelf, and paying by credit card at the cash register is sheer fantasy to most of the world's population. (As one Honduran told me, there would be nothing left on the shelf within days, merely because of theft.)

Many teens have never had any close relationships with adults. This is why so many adults find it difficult to talk to teens, who often seem to want to be somewhere else talking to someone else. But in many ways, teens want to please adults, so they often behave the way they *think* adults want them to behave. This way of thinking, however, easily leads to habits of deception. Students have an incredible ability to "fake it," and appearing a certain way in front of their parents and teachers and a different way in front of their friends is an accepted part of the teen culture. When confronted by an adult, denying, even lying, is normal. Ratting on friends is the most certain way to be ostracized by peers, and even the best students are unlikely to report unhealthy or dangerous behavior to anyone in authority. Parents who try to establish rules are inevitably compared with more lax parents. In spite of the fact that everyone needs boundaries, teens continually push for less accountability. "Don't you trust me?" they say, even though they do much to make adults mistrust them.

When kids have parents that are at work when the kids come home from school, and when kids can go places where they are not responsible to adults, there are far fewer opportunities for a teenager to learn responsibility from adults. And as America has become an increasingly suburban nation, it has become more difficult for parents to give children responsible tasks. At the time of the Great Depression, only 26.6 percent of the population lived in the city.[1] In rural America young children gathered eggs, older children milked cows, and teenagers performed the work of an adult. However, it wasn't the difficulty of the work as much as the responsibility that had the effect of helping the young family member to mature. The family depended on the work being done by the child. Therefore, the child was an integral and important part of the family, and this helped give the child the self-image of being a significant contributor.

When today's students work, and many of them do, they almost always work outside of the home in low-skilled service jobs where quality or quantity of work is difficult to measure. In fact, for many such jobs, a winsome personality and good hustle is nearly all that is needed for success.

I have asked so many students, "What does your father or mother do?"

I get answers such as, "My father works in a bank."

"Well, what does he do?" I ask again.

"I'm not sure. I think he works in the loan department."

"What does he do in the loan department?"

"I'm not sure, but I think he makes loans. It's a very responsible position. He works very hard."

Such conversations indicate to me that most students have no idea what their parents actually do or what is involved in their workday. It is extremely rare to find a student who has spent one day with his father or mother doing what they do; many have never been in either parent's workplace. The word "responsibility," therefore, has little meaning. They have found that when they mess up or don't know how to do something, it is best to be winsome. (When students are doing poorly in a class, they often look for ways to beat the system rather than study harder.)

When higher education began to explode, the educational leaders were all familiar with the depression and World War II. Many of the assumptions of modern education are built on assumptions regarding student maturity and responsibility that are no longer valid. The typical student entering college has never been given the responsibility for doing something in a certain way, by a specific time, and for a specific amount of money. Students of previous generations knew that when things are done improperly, there can be serious consequences —a missile blowing up, a buddy being wounded, having to get married, etc. Most of today's students are shielded from the serious, undesirable consequences of irresponsible behavior. The obvious exceptions are getting AIDS or having a serious car accident.

With so little life experience, many students mature slowly and have little confidence in their competency. Instead, they try to please adults by acting the way they perceive others want them to act—friendly, respectful, and energetic. I'm not trained in psychology, but this lack of competency seems to be a leading contributor to two other common teenage characteristics that I've observed: obsessive-compulsive behavior and passive-aggressive behavior. Obsessive-compulsive behavior results in constant activity, the need always to be doing something. Most kids find it difficult to be alone, to meditate, or to contemplate on abstract things. It is not surprising to me that so many kids have attention deficit disorders and must take drugs like Ritalin. They are simply too busy trying to please others, and perhaps this desire to please stems from their lack of experience and competency. This, in turn, contributes to low self-confidence.

Furthermore, many teens are passive-aggressive. Their external pleasantness hides a lot of internal insecurity, resentment, and anger. They have built-up hostility and anger, but they don't know how to deal with it. They know that they should not be outwardly belligerent, so they hold in their feelings. When they get mad, they are more likely to "get even" than to get vocally or visibly angry. This is why so many teenagers withdraw into the privacy of their room or their peer group, where they can attempt to either distract themselves with entertainment or vent their feelings with sympathetic friends. Of course, neither of these types of activities deals with the real problem. The feeling of anger is not resolved this way, and teens continue in the pattern of behavior that led to the problem in the first place.

Television and Computers

If you spend any time with kids, the conversation will inevitably center on movies, television shows, and songs. Kids relate more on the basis of what they have *seen* than what they have *done.* Much of the national "language" of college students emits from mass communications. Thus, what they have in common is not playing a sport, working, going to church, etc. What they have in common is knowing the same songs, seeing the same movies, watching the same television shows. All of these so-called common experiences that form the basis for relationships are fictitious representations of the world. Television and movies have shaped their view of the world; they have spent far more hours in front of the television than they have studying.

We live in an entertainment era. More than ever, visual electronics—movies, television, and computers—shape our view of the world. They provide news, documentary, drama, and comedy all at the same time, according to what you select. Someone coined the word "infotainment." Infotainment may be seeing a talk on poverty, followed by a commercial selling hairspray, a documentary on the rise of Hitler, and a sporting event, all in the span of a few minutes.

To the mind uninformed by real-life experiences, there is little capacity to differentiate between the various types of television shows: news, documentary, drama, entertainment, etc. The thousands of images—from seeing actual murders to seeing two people make love—powerfully influence the way we think the world really works.

In one instance, television vividly showed us the potential danger of an electronic world. When a sailor on a U.S. warship saw a plane on the radar screen and the plane was shot down, crewmen later found that the plane was not an enemy aircraft but rather a commercial airliner. The sailor did not even see the airplane—if he had, he would have known that it was not a fighter plane. The sailor only saw a visual image on a screen. In addition, senseless high school killings show us that many teenagers have a hard time differentiating between the real world and electronic images.

In the mid-eighties, it was uncommon for students to have televisions or computers in their rooms. Now nearly every student has a computer or television or both. Students used to spend time in their rooms studying, sleeping, or talking. Now students spend a lot of time in front of these electronic machines (often alone and sometimes with a friend). Some of their time on the computer is related to homework. Students can legitimately do research in their own room on the Internet, and they can write papers on the computer. The Internet also allows faculty to communicate easily with students and give assignments. But the computer and television are used mostly to play a computer game, write or read a message, surf the net, watch an old movie, or watch MTV.

There was a day when teachers did not have so much infotainment competition, when it was easier to emphasize learning. But I think students today are less likely to read and more likely to see things in a superficial way. Increasingly, students are staying in their own rooms and not even interacting with other students. Student development personnel have begun to talk of computer addiction. Combined with few opportunities to hold responsibility and less parenting, television has led students to believe that it is easier to find solutions to problems than is actually the case. Furthermore, the solutions the student sees on television are often more fantasy than reality.

Even televised college events contribute to this fantasy. Students who don't even play intramural sports become, *in their minds*, "fighting Irishmen" or "Tar Heels." This is complete fantasy; most students have never gone through even a single week of rigorous physical training, much less the years of training that Division-One college athletes undergo. (And if you really want to know how bad the fantasy is, see how many students watch the lesser-known live contests in minor events such as college baseball, tennis, swimming, etc. Such major intercollegiate events often will attract less than fifty people.) It is not surprising that national studies on physical fitness indicate a continuing decline in the health of young people, even as the popularity of spectator sports is increasing. Students enjoy vicariously what they are not able to enjoy in fact because they are unwilling to take the time and effort to become athletically competent themselves. This spectator mentality bleeds into academic endeavors.

Television and videos make it much harder to teach students to write a paper without grammatical errors, to comprehend tables of complicated data, or to consider important ideas and their consequences. In short, television makes it harder to get students to engage in the slow process of learning. In the real world after college, there will be real problems requiring real solutions. The infotainment world of electronic media will not have prepared most students for this world.

Sex and Alcohol

Educators talk about the before-five culture and the after-five culture. The party environment on college campuses is a real threat to the learning environment, and sex is a pervasive influence on the college campus. It is hard to "shock" the average student. There is no such thing as being discreet. Students talk openly about condoms, sexually explicit movies, and sexual acts, even sexual acts once considered weird and unnatural. They are unashamed about public displays of affection; it is not at all uncommon to walk into a lounge and see a male and female student lying down together on a couch. Sexual intercourse with multiple partners is common. For many young people, having sex is considered a natural biological function between two consenting adults; most students feel there is nothing wrong with consensual sex. Love and sex are not equated. Terms have developed such as "sport sex," evidence that sex has become a game for many young people. It is easy to have sex without a relationship. At the same time, it is difficult to have a relationship without sex. This leads many students to avoid "dating" altogether, because once they start dating, they get into a world complicated by sexual expectations.

Not all sex is a result of alcohol abuse, but drinking and sex certainly go together. Binge drinking—drinking to get drunk—is very prevalent. The Harvard School of Public Health College Alcohol Study, 1999, reported that 44 percent of college students are binge drinkers. A high percentage of college presidents say that alcohol abuse is the number one problem on campus. A nondrinking student told me of visiting an 8:00 class at another college where the students were obviously half-asleep and hungover. No matter how hard the professor tried to engage the students, he could get no response. Most teachers know the difficulty of teaching early morning classes, and many try to avoid them.

Because of the difficulty of controlling both sex and alcohol in college residence halls, many campuses have allowed much of the housing to be built by private developers. Students are treated as adults who can live where they please and do what they please, as long as they meet the academic requirements. Many colleges have completely abandoned the idea of trying to create a "learning environment" where what goes on out of the classroom supports what is going on in the classroom.

Of course, the attraction to the opposite sex goes along with the age group. Dealing with alcohol is not a new problem either. However, twenty-five years ago there were many more rules to keep these matters within boundaries that protected the learning environment. Now the norm among college students is promiscuous sex accompanied by excessive drinking. In many housing complexes there is a party almost every night. Sexually transmitted diseases are at epidemic levels. One student described to her professor her relationship with the friend she was going out with by saying, "It's just all about sex." The social scene is so complicated and distracting that many students are so absorbed by their various personal emotions and interactions that they cannot properly focus on the material they are supposed to be studying.

The problem is deeper than merely a distraction from studies, however. College men and women who treat sex so casually and who use alcohol so freely to enhance their social interaction lose their sense of self-worth. Once the most intimate sexual acts are equated with meeting biological urges, a person begins to view his or her own body as being ordinary and common. A lower sense of self-worth tends to lead to lower self-expectations.

Many students develop a "get by" attitude as a result. They do not see themselves as being courageous or virtuous. They do not think they will ever do anything important. They have minimalist expectations—a job they like, relatively good health, and a partner they can get along with. Most students do not view themselves as hardworking, creative, motivated, or ambitious, and success is generally equated with material success.

So the sexually promiscuous party scene that lets people use one another for their own lusts is robbing students not only of their innocence but of their hopes and dreams. It is turning students from being idealistic about making a better world to being obsessed by fun, sex, and drugs. Many students are cynical. They don't think they can make a difference; often they don't even have that aspiration. In fact, many have a strong suspicion of leaders and don't associate virtuous character traits with success. Politicians are all crooks; businessmen are all money-grubbers; athletes and movie stars have to use drugs to make it; clerics use religion for their own ends to promote their own biases. Most students don't feel they know "successful" people. Though many of their images of success are obviously television stereotypes, they still reject nearly all role models—not just public role models but even their parents and their teachers.

But sometimes there is reason for this rejection. The person behind the persona has disillusioned many students who have met "successful" people. One of my colleagues still recalls his own disillusionment when one night at 2:00 A.M. he met a renowned middle-aged visiting scholar, drunk, trying to pick up a twenty-year-old coed. Such disillusionment is common, and in the midst of this, it is difficult to get students to aspire to lofty goals. The learning environment is very different when the prevailing mood is one of cynical self-interest as opposed to youthful idealism.

This cynicism carries over into the realm of marriage. College students talk openly about the advantages and disadvantages of being married versus living together. They talk about learning if they are compatible with someone, not about getting married. With the average marriage age being twenty-seven, marriage is something that occurs in the distant future, at least in most students' minds. They think even less about having children; they might talk about having children when they talk about marriage, but it is seldom an important aspiration of college students. (They also see themselves as having a small family—children are expensive. They believe this, I think, because they have heard it from their parents: Too many children will limit your ability to take nice vacations or have nice things.)

All of these reasons contribute to the fact that, though getting a college degree is important if a student wants a good job, starting a family or a career seems to be in the distant future. Doing well in school so that they can get married, have children, and start a career was a dream of many students years ago; it is not the dream of today's students.

Students have sometimes described life after college as "the job thing," and they are in no hurry to get to that place. They know it's coming, but they don't anticipate the "real world." This may sound contradictory with the earlier comment that students are more likely to view college as preparation for a job than as preparation for life. Students do go to college to get a good job and to earn more money. To them, this beats the alternative of doing work they don't like for low pay. Work is work; no one likes it. If they are going to do something they don't like, they might as well at least get paid well, and that is why they go to college. Still, they don't rush into the work world with any enthusiasm.

College offices of career counseling advise students to get jobs they will like and be good at. There is little emphasis on doing what college should be doing: Teaching students things they don't know so that they will be able to perform at a much higher level of competency. Rather than taking courses where they are manifestly weak, students take courses where they know they are strong. They do not see the value of developing weaknesses, and they do not pursue courses to that end.

Religion

Students are often religious. America is the most religious country in the industrial world, and participation in formal religious organizations is very high compared to other countries. The following is how year 2000 freshmen identified themselves.

Fall 2000 Freshmen

Religion/Denomination	Percent
Baptist	11.6
Buddhist	1.0
Eastern Orthodox	.7
Episcopal	1.7
Islamic	.9
Jewish	2.8
Mormon	1.5
Lutheran	5.8
Methodist	6.4
Presbyterian	4.0
Quaker	.2
Roman Catholic	30.5
Seventh Day Adventist	.3
United Church of Christ	1.5
Other Christians	12.7
Other	3.6
None	14.9

Data is from *The American Freshman National Norms for Fall 2000* (Los Angeles: Higher Education Research Institute, UCLA, 2000).

While Americans tend to be as religious as ever, and students are no exception, the level of biblical knowledge is far less than it used to be.[2] Those who work in large college-campus ministries, such as Campus Crusade and InterVarsity or Reformed University Ministries, have told me that they can no longer assume students will have even a rudimentary knowledge of biblical concepts such as sin and atonement. Even those who go to seminary are often biblically illiterate. For instance, four out of ten college students cannot tell you how many disciples Jesus had.[3]

Since people are inherently religious, students are vulnerable to religious fads. Along with the increasing number of those interested in world religions such as Hinduism and Islam has come an increase in those interested in cults ranging from Satan worship to New Age religion. Most students seem to think that religious beliefs are not held to the same tests for validity as other beliefs. Religious beliefs are thought to be expressions of personal belief.

Religion is the expression of what a person believes to be of ultimate importance. Although people do not always follow their religious convictions, this does not mean that their convictions are unimportant. But what this does mean for college students is that they bring to the classroom a hodgepodge of untested beliefs about the world. There is not much likelihood that these beliefs can be articulated, and if they could be articulated, most likely they would not form a coherent picture.

With students possessing such incoherent and varied worldviews, it is very difficult for the professor to know where to start teaching a class. This is why students seem to be "in their own world," a world that adults do not recognize or know how to communicate with.

As with other changes, it is hard to know the precise impact of promiscuity, role expectations, alcohol, prosperity, inexperience, lack of adult contact, and religious ignorance. However, I am confident that these social changes make it far harder to get eighteen- to twenty-one-year-old students to concentrate on their studies than was the case fifty years ago.

Conclusion

I am writing from my observations, experience, and reading in the field of education. In order to make this a parent-friendly book that is easily readable, I have intentionally not tried to "prove my case" with copious references. Certainly, not all students are alike, and many students do not fit the descriptions above. But there is much research on the subjects mentioned, so at the end of this book I have a list for further reading if you are interested in doing so. To conclude this chapter, I will also show a few figures that give some indication of the extent to which students do fit the descriptions I have given.

Attitudes and Characteristics of Freshmen
at Four-Year Colleges, Fall 2000

Objectives considered essential or very important [top 5 and bottom 5]:	%
Being very well-off financially	73.4
Raising a family	73.1
Helping others who are in difficulty	61.7
Becoming an authority in my field	59.7
Obtaining recognition from my colleagues for contributions to my field	51.4
Becoming involved in programs to clean up the environment	17.5
Making a theoretical contribution to science	16.0
Creating artistic work	14.8
Writing original works	14.7
Being accomplished in the performing arts	14.5

Reasons noted as very important in deciding to go to college [top 5]:	%
To learn more about things that interest me	76.6
To get training for a specific career	71.8
To be able to get a better job	71.6
To be able to make more money	70.0
To gain a general education and appreciation of ideas	64.5

Reasons noted as very important in selecting college attended [top 4 and bottom 4]	%
College has a good academic reputation	53.9
Graduates get good jobs	50.3
Size of college	34.4
Offered financial assistance	33.8
Not accepted anywhere else	2.9
Teacher's advice	4.3
Recruited by college	4.5
Not offered aid by first choice	5.2

Figures taken from "Attitudes and Characteristics of Freshmen,"
The Chronicle of Higher Education (fall 1997): 22.

To summarize, nearly three-fourths of college freshmen at the tender age of eighteen want to be well-off financially, so they decide to go to college. The two main reasons students select a particular college is because the college has a good academic reputation and because graduates get good jobs—two criteria closely related in students' minds. Freshmen seek money and success!

4

Helping Students Ask the Right Questions

Adults who try to help students choose a college need to help students develop appropriate skills.

- Students need to be encouraged to make choices based on principle.
- Students need to be encouraged to think.
- Students need to communicate—to talk seriously about serious things.
- Students need to relate to all kinds of people without having to give up principle.

All of these skills must be *learned*. It is obvious from this list that to learn these things, kids need love and attention from their parents. Most readers are probably aware of surveys that show the small amount of meaningful time that parents spend with students. Usually the surveys show that parents and teenagers have less than two or three minutes of meaningful contact on a daily basis. I assume that spending meaningful time means having an extended conversation about an important subject or doing something together—not simply sharing a meal or watching television. Spending meaningful time might include reviewing homework and discussing errors made, not just asking about grades. Spending meaningful time might include working together on a project, not just having family members independently fulfilling their individual household chores. Part of this lack of time spent together must be the result of more two-working-parent families, in which the parents have less time to spend with their children. Often what children need is time; what parents give is time in day-care centers, after-school activities, summer camps, etc.

Not only does love and time affect a child's ability to make choices but so does adult trust. Does the adult trust the child enough to allow the child to make the decision? Expectations have profound results. If you expect a child to act responsibly, the child is more likely to act responsibly than if you expect a child to act irresponsibly. However, the child will not always act responsibly, and the parent will often be disappointed. But children learn from their choices.

I know of a family in which the parents had high expectations of their children. They talked to their children about the importance of a college education as early as the seventh grade and told them that they would probably not be able to contribute much toward that education because of limited resources. So instead the parents encouraged each child to begin saving money toward college. All five children of varying ability received at least part of their education from Covenant, which cost more at the time the students were enrolled than what the family made when the topic of college was first introduced.

It must be kept in mind, however, that parents need to emphasize the importance of college for *some* students. Not all students are college material. And parents also need to be careful with what *kind* of expectations they have for their children. Sadly, many parents seem more interested in telling their friends that their child got a scholarship to brand X prestigious college (or athletic program) than in their child's well-being.

I encourage parents of young children to aim to have children ready to live independently by the age of eighteen. In other words, by the time the child reaches the traditional college age, he or she should be able to live away from his or her parents. I always told my children that when they were eighteen they would have to join the military, spend a year in missions, get a job, or go to college. They would not be allowed to live at home without contributing financially. If they went to college, I told them that they should go away to college. My second child actually went to Covenant, only three miles from home, but she was not allowed to come home except for breaks during her first year.

But even if parents do their best to prepare their child for independence, not all students are mature enough to go off to college, especially boys. If a child does not want to go to college, I often encourage parents to let the child get some work experience or do something in the form of a missions project in which he or she will learn to serve others. It is surprising how a year of routine physical labor and low pay can reorder a child's priorities. However, if parents plan ahead to prepare children to live independently by the age of eighteen, most students will relish the idea of going off to college. And attending a college that challenges the student to grow in maturity and responsibility is excellent preparation for being entirely self-sufficient by the time of graduation.

For some parents, helping students make wise choices is tantamount to abrogation of any role in the process. Parents who merely assume that their children will go to college, but who do not communicate *why* a student should go to college or *how* a student needs to grow in order to succeed in college, often fail their children by unwarranted trust. As a result, too many kids look at college as the best way to prolong adolescence. Going off with friends to a place where there are no rules and where parents continue to pay the bills sounds like a dream. Sadly, only about one-third of all students who go to college end up graduating from that college within the normal time. College dropout is a national embarrassment and a huge cost in terms of both money and lost potential. But this is only the most visible part of the problem. Many students learn to beat the system, to graduate without really getting the benefits of a good education. For them, the college taught that they could pass with last-minute cramming and cheating or by taking crip courses and easy majors.

Even wise and caring parents who are committed to guiding their children still agonize over how to help. I think I know why.

Some years ago, Covenant College retained the services of a communications firm to help us conduct some focus groups. On three occasions in three different cities, we gathered for about two hours in a room with approximately a dozen parents of college-bound kids. A trained questioner asked a series of preplanned questions. We were not surprised to learn that there was a high degree of consensus concerning the basics of a good education: small classes, competent teachers (who could serve as mentors), a wholesome environment, etc. When the focus group was over, we felt that the parents had described Covenant College. All we had to do was to tell our story. But we asked one more question: "Where are your children planning to go?" The responses shocked us. All of the students were going either to community colleges, large state universities, or prestigious research universities.

We extended the sessions. We asked:
"Do you think they will have small classes?"
"No."
"Do you think students will get to know their teachers, that the teachers could serve as mentors?"
"No."
"Do you think it is a wholesome environment?"
"No."
"Well, why is your child going there?" we asked somewhat incredulously.
"Because, with a degree from there, my child can get a good job."

When it came down to making a decision, parents seemed more concerned about their child getting a good job than a good education. It is a serious mistake for parents to tell children that the main reason to go to college is so that they can make a better living. It may be true, but it is not a sufficient reason for going to college.

Jesus said, whoever saves his life will lose it and whoever loses his life will save it. Said another way, if we would not die for something, we will not experience life. Our forefathers literally died for freedom; in so doing, they lived, and we are the beneficiaries. We have freedom. Is success or excellence the same as virtue? If we say to our children that the most important thing is to get a good job, their interpretation is "So you don't come back and live with us; we have spent all we can spend on you. You need to take care of yourself now, but someday, you will need to take care of us." If we say that going to college, i.e., making money, is more important than happiness, honesty, self-respect, a good education, or learning to live (rather than make a living), we are selling our kids short. We are giving them nothing to die for; therefore, they will not fully experience life.

But having said this, I also realize the difficult choices that you as a parent have to make. Let me try to walk you through some of this difficult terrain.

Reputation

There is no doubt that some colleges' reputation is such that a degree from them will open doors. But of the 2,100 four-year nonprofit colleges, how many are known for giving excellent educations? Unless a student is extremely gifted, choosing a prestigious college will not be an issue for most parents of most children. There are literally only a hundred or less colleges that have such an outstanding reputation.

For parents who attach great significance to the prestige of the college, I would suggest you remember that even the most prestigious colleges have many alumni who have not been "successful," so going to a famous college does not guarantee success. The only time that anyone really cares where you went to college is when you get your first job. After that, what is important is your job performance. Furthermore, there is ample evidence that college reputation cannot be equated with quality education. Many schools enjoy a good reputation long after ceasing to provide a good education. Many other schools striving to provide a good education have not yet gained the reputation they deserve. Reputation is so vague.

Each year I am asked by *U.S. News & World Report* to rank schools in my region. Even as a college president,

I am embarrassed by the subjectivity of my own evaluations. I am unfamiliar with most colleges, even those in my own region. I realize that some successful people did go to prestigious colleges, but when I've talked to those people, sometimes I feel that more of their success can be attributed to their intelligence and motivation than to their education. For the Christian, pride is never a good motivation. It is more important to graduate knowing that you have to prove your ability than to graduate thinking that you are God's gift to the world and employers would be fortunate to have you as an employee. I had a boss who used to introduce me by saying, "Frank went to Harvard Business School, but he'll get over it." I began to appreciate what he was trying to teach me.

Obviously, I am not saying that reputation is of no importance. The reputation of a college simply must be kept in its proper perspective. The students who can get into the prestigious colleges are those most likely to go to graduate school. Yet graduate schools are accustomed to admitting students from all types of colleges, not just the few prestigious colleges everyone knows. In fact, prestigious graduate schools have lots of students from less-than-prestigious colleges. If these prestigious graduate schools have so many students from less-well-known colleges, how great should a parent's concern be for the prestige of the undergraduate school?

The concern about prestige is often a misguided concern about the quality of education. When I press parents on why they think a particular school is excellent, I find that they seldom know who the president is; they don't know many students who went to the school; they don't know any professors who teach there. About all they know is that the school is hard to get into and it's expensive. I suspect that many of the schools who say they only take one out of eight students who apply attract students who apply to eight selective schools. The pool of highly gifted students is probably about the same size as the enrollment of these highly selective schools. Some colleges are actually fearful of being too cheap, because they fear they will be perceived as offering an inferior college education. If my math is correct, some schools have more employees than students and have enough endowments to provide everyone full tuition, but they still have outrageously high tuition. I wish parents would not assume that cost equals prestige, which equals quality.

The Learning Environment

Everything I have read indicates that most of the things people consider in choosing a college are irrelevant to the existence of a learning environment. Let's put it this way. I don't think there is a statistical correlation between the existence of a learning environment and any of the following: size of the college, reputation of the college, endowment of the college, cost of the college, religious nature of the college, location of the college, age of the college, or ranking of the college.

When meeting with school personnel, the adults often ask the questions they think the student should ask. "Ashley is very interested in literature. Can you tell us about your English major?" I often get the impression that Ashley has entirely different questions that she never gets to ask. It is important to prepare your children for college tours and to get them to ask questions even if you are present.

If you really want to find a school with a learning environment, you are going to have to evaluate that yourself, and this is not that hard to do. Attend classes. Try to get the child to observe the following things:

Was there interaction between the students and the professor in the class?

Did students appear interested or bored?

Were students taking notes?

What are tests like? Are they true/false and fill in the blank, or essay tests?

Have your son or daughter spend a night in the dorm. This is another important way to see if there is real learning going on. Teach your children to ask themselves:

What do students talk about when they are not in class? Do they ever talk about what they are supposedly learning? If not, why not?

What do students do when they are not in class? Do they talk on a personal level or a theoretical level? Does there seem to be real engagement with the world of ideas?

Do students seem to have favorite courses and professors? Why? What are they learning from the teacher and the class?

How much homework are students doing each day?

Are there places to go where it is conducive to studying? How about the dorms? Are they party houses or residence halls where friends live responsibly, helping one another in constructive ways?

Do I like this college? What do I like about it? Does it have anything to do with learning, or do I like the school mainly because of the students who go there and the things to do unrelated to academics?

What do students do on the weekend? Is this a 24/7 learning environment, or is this a commuter college with learning during the week only? Are students involved in campus life and community life? Is this really a community of learners?

It is not that hard to tell if there is a learning environment. You might even go so far as to tell your child that you will pay for college only if you are convinced that there is a learning environment, and explain why you are so insistent on such an environment.

The Pew Trusts sponsored a 3.3 million dollar project called the National Survey of Student Engagement. The purpose of the survey of 276 institutions was to gauge the extent to which colleges encourage learning. More than 63,000 students filled out the 40-question survey. The report, "Improving the College Experience," is only 36 pages long and is well worth reading in its entirety (www.ivb.edu/~nsse). The survey even differentiated between liberal arts colleges, general colleges, master's colleges, doctoral-intensive universities, etc., so that they were not comparing apples and oranges.

The nature of the student experience varies greatly both between and in the institutional sectors and types. Looking at benchmark scores of the highest and lowest institutions, the range of academic challenge for seniors is about 22% (22 points) of the 100 point scale. For enriching educational experiences for first-year students the range is 40 points.[1] The benchmarks used are: level of academic challenge, active and collaborative learning, student interaction with faculty, enriching educational experiences, and supportive campus environment. These benchmarks describe well the idea of a "learning environment."

Some say that such a survey may be a better approach to measuring institutional quality.

The Chronicle of Higher Education reported highlights of some of the questions, the types of questions that you also may want to ask (see pages 136–37). You need to learn to ask perceptive questions about the learning environment and teach your child to do the same. Does the college have an environment that encourages such learning? How can you tell? You may get a response from kids that it is not "cool" to be a "geek," but you need to emphasize the importance of learning, the sheer joy of learning, and the great benefits of learning.[2] Learning dramatically goes up when the student is *involved* in the learning process, because learning is not a passive exercise.

So look for a college that has a learning environment that encourages student involvement, because there is great disparity between colleges in this regard. The survey researcher said, "One surprise was that some high-profile schools don't do as well as some schools that most people have never heard of."[3] Don't let your child be surprised by the lack of a learning environment.

Religious Aspects

Some years ago, I was on the board of the Council of Christian Colleges, and we retained the services of a marketing firm to help us understand the perception of Christian colleges. We learned that Bob Jones, Notre Dame, and Texas Christian University were among the better-known Christian colleges. The fact that these three universities have very different ways of looking at the role of religion in education leads me to conclude that we must look beyond religious labels.

In my mind there seem to be several categories of religious colleges:

1. historically religious colleges with almost no continuing influence of religion on faculty-hiring or the curriculum

2. church-related colleges that are nominally religious, where more of the faculty may profess faith but where there is little impact on the course offerings or core courses
3. colleges where the religious influence is pervasive and affects hiring decisions and curriculum design
4. colleges that seem more concerned with protection and indoctrination than with education

To further complicate this picture, of those colleges with a pervasive religious influence, there are colleges that are theologically liberal or conservative, denominational or nondenominational, small or large, academically weak or strong, with strict or loose rules, selective or open admissions, and a national or local student-body composition. It is terribly complicated, to say the least.

My philosophy on how to choose is to consider things in this order:

Don't even consider religious affiliation if the college is only historically or nominally religious. Consider it a secular college.

Don't make your child go to a religious college. It usually backfires. He or she should want to go.

Look for a learning environment. Make sure the academic rigor is there! Make sure the school is serious about education and is not attracting students mainly on the basis of religious fervor or commitment. Check out the caliber of students and make sure your child would fit in.

Make sure there is a strong core and that the religious content is in classes, not just in chapel. The faculty, not just the chaplain, must be strong in their faith. Remember, you are choosing a college, not a church.

Avoid colleges whose theology is opposite your own.

Choose a school that lets students grow up, not one with so many rules that it postpones the inevitable. Students must learn to make wise choices. That means they must go to a college that lets them make poor choices, but that also helps them understand the consequences of those choices and learn from the experience. Remember, no college can "protect" your child. The youth culture of any campus is not a "safe" environment. In fact, education is inherently dangerous; ideas are dangerous. My experience is that even on very religious campuses a student has to doubt his or her inherited faith and go through a period of questioning before coming to grips with what he or she personally believes.

Look for a good matchup in terms of size. Some students will thrive on a large campus; others need a small campus.

Don't believe that Christian education is automatically inferior or that it is poor preparation for the "real world." This is not so. It especially grieves me that so many dads seem to think that a religious college would be good for their daughter but that their son needs to go to a big secular school. Nothing could be farther from the truth. Girls are often more mature than boys are at the same age and seem to be able to make wiser choices. If anyone needs what religious schools offer, it is the boys.

In 1968 more than 80 percent of all students thought developing a meaningful philosophy of life was important; by 1990 less than half of all students thought developing a meaningful philosophy of life was important. By 1990 more than 70 percent of freshmen listed "be well-off financially" as an important college goal.[4]

Even if students don't see college as a place where they develop a meaningful philosophy of life, this should be an important goal. If the main purpose for selecting a religious college is to help students develop a sense of meaning and purpose, then making a living is also fulfilling. Too many students believe that they have "to work to eat" and "eat to work." Such circular reasoning ultimately leads to disillusionment or even depression.

When comparing the benefits of Christian colleges to secular colleges, many parents find encouragement in the fact that many secular colleges have excellent religious student groups on campus. These ministries can help religious students in important ways. However, if the student is constantly being taught from a secular perspective in the classroom, an undesirable consequence can be a compartmentalization of faith, so that one considers faith irrelevant to what one "knows."

The purpose of a Christian college should be to educate students so that they will have an informed faith, one that is based on knowledge of religious choices that one has and needs to consider. While parachurch groups on the secular campus can provide a safe haven for Christians to do this, students should not be under the illusion that they are gaining a college-level knowledge of how Scripture relates to the academic disciplines. On the other hand, students and parents need to recognize that faith is personal, and going to a Christian college cannot substitute for personal commitment to gaining biblical knowledge and applying it.

Students should get their knowledge of the Bible from someone who believes the Bible to be inspired and authoritative. In evaluating a Christian college, it is important to assess the college's attitude toward the inspiration and authority of Scripture.

Selectivity

Students encourage or discourage one another. It is important for your child to be among students who will challenge him or her academically. There must be a reasonable number of similarly gifted students to challenge your student. However, everyone does not have to be gifted; even three or four gifted students in a class will motivate one another and will motivate the rest of the class.

Colleges are rated according to selectivity. I am a little suspicious of some of the ways this information is created. As previously noted, the most gifted students are the ones that make multiple applications to the most-difficult-to-get-into colleges. Therefore, I have always questioned the validity of the "percent-accepted" figures. There are other reliable numbers indicating high school performance and SAT scores. In the case of SAT scores, you should ask not only for averages but also for the averages of each quartile. For example, the average SAT could be 1200, with the top quartile averaging 1400 and the bottom quartile averaging 1000. If you had a child with a 1400 SAT, you could be sure that he or she would be challenged.

Cost

College recruiting specialists say that most people write off private colleges without further investigation because of the cost. My advice is, don't do this. Go through the financial-aid process and make your decision after all the information is in.

There are a few things you should know. The average family income at private colleges is almost the same as at public colleges. The most expensive decision is to trade a good education for a cheap education. It is like

buying poor quality of anything else, except worse—
you may be stuck with a bad education the rest of your
life. I will deal more fully with financial aid in the next
chapter.

The Role of a College Where There Is Community

There are some very good large universities that get
good students and have good learning environments. But
don't mistake size for quality. Bigness does not necessarily mean goodness. My own son transferred to Covenant
College from a large prestigious university and was surprised to find a community where learning was valued
even more than at the research university. Furthermore,
he found a community that was far more supportive of
personal application.

With larger colleges often comes the loss of a sense
of community. The idea of a learning community that
is primarily shaped by the college is usually a myth for
college students in large schools. Sixty-four percent of
students go to college within one hundred miles of
their home, while only 8.3 percent attend college more
than five hundred miles from home.[5] The result is that
many colleges, even those with a large residential population, become commuter colleges where a large percent of the student body clears out on weekends. This
makes it very difficult for the college to establish a
"learning community."

One way that a community is defined is by commonly
held convictions about what is important. Moral standards help form community, but if you judge colleges
by their moral codes, then colleges fail the test of being
communities. Often the closest thing to a moral stan-
dard is the idea of "tolerance."

Because of widespread discrimination, many colleges have adopted ethical codes that encourage greater tolerance of certain groups. But merely acknowledging the need for people of different cultures to live peacefully in close physical proximity does not necessarily make a community. The attempt of school policies to force tolerance often backfires. Students are very suspicious of these codes; they learn to watch what they say, but their biases are not fundamentally affected. "Political correctness" is a threat to real community.

In absence of moral standards or ethics, universities often try to substitute the desire for academic "excellence," but this term remains undefined. "Excellence" does not mean a common learning experience; it does not mean academic rigor; it does not mean a community devoted to learning. For instance, while cheating is universally condemned, it is widely practiced. Often excellence refers to excellence of facilities, excellence of faculty credentials, excellence of resources. But being rich and famous is not the same as being virtuous, and excellence without virtue is a hollow concept.

Often there are two cultures on a campus, a before-five culture dominated by those employed by the college, and an after-five culture dominated by students. Even college-sponsored activities designed purely for student entertainment often fail to obtain student interest. Especially in large schools, most students do not participate in college-sponsored clubs or activities. Major college sporting events become spectator events, and the students often don't even personally know the players. So social life occurs outside of the purview of the college administration—often in local restaurants, recreation centers, malls, bars, and especially in students' apartments. It is not unusual for most students to live off campus in private housing, where students can do anything they want.

Mentally, students create a lot of distance between their private lives and the college. They "go" to the college to take classes and, perhaps, to use the library. They come "home" to study. They go out with their college friends nearby. In other words, many students regard the college as a place to go to get what they want, much like going to a mall. *Newsweek* characterized today's colleges as "giant youth preserves." "Adolescents want to do everything sooner—everything but grow up."[6]

"Fewer than one in six of all undergraduates fit the traditional stereotype of the American college student attending full-time, being 18–22 years of age, and living on campus."[7] There is little sense of community that encourages staying in college. In spite of the relatively high number of students who enroll in college, only 34.2 percent of the 1998–99 beginning post secondary students had attained a bachelor's degree by 1994. According to the most recent census data, only 25.6 percent of adults age twenty-five and older have a bachelor's degree or a degree higher than a bachelor's degree.[8] The attitude that is more prevalent than the idea of going to college and graduating in four years is to "check out" a college. Often students hardly know themselves what year they are in. The words "freshman," "sophomore," "junior," and "senior" are used less often. More common is an expression such as, "I've been here two years."[9]

Conclusion

Yes, choosing a college is a lot of work, and it is complicated! How do you decide on the relative importance of reputation, learning environment, religious aspects, selectivity, cost, size, and community? You learn to think on the basis of principles. And this is precisely why your role is important. By helping the student think through the issues carefully, you are helping prepare that student in the most important way—by teaching the student why he or she must be committed to learning. Students need to recognize that they need what college can provide, but they also need to learn that it won't happen by just going to college. The student must be committed to wanting to learn! And you play an important role in helping the student come to this conclusion.

5

Practical Essentials in Making the College Choice

Your immediate goal in beginning a college search is to select no more than ten schools to visit so that the student can apply to four to six colleges or universities. In order to best do this, you will want to seek the counsel of others, especially professional college placement counselors, if they are competent, trustworthy, and available. You will want to talk to students and parents of students who may know a school better than you do. You may want to buy a college guide. Consider some of the specialized guides such as those on Christian colleges or liberal arts colleges. Search the Internet. All colleges have web sites that are very informative, and there are college guidance web sites as well. (You might want to use the College Board web site, which is www.collegeboard.org.) Most colleges will have their course offerings, their student discipline policies, and much more information about the college on their web site.

It is a good idea to have a student take the PSAT in the tenth grade and the SAT early in the eleventh grade (see chapter nine for more about preparing a student for college) so that you will have an indication of the student's ability to take standardized tests. Some colleges prefer the ACT and others the SAT. Many will accept either. Most colleges can give you a range of the test scores of entering students that will help you be realistic in terms of the schools you consider. If a child does not test well, you may want to consider colleges that don't require standardized tests but use other methods to evaluate students. Most schools use a variety of indicators such as GPA, standardized test scores, essays, high school transcripts, references, reputation of the high school, advanced placement scores, etc. Most schools will give you some idea of what they weigh most heavily, but few schools will tell you how they actually weigh all elements. Nevertheless, you need to know your student's strengths and weaknesses, and you must evaluate these in comparison to what a particular college values, in order to screen out certain colleges.

Establish Priorities

As you begin your research, the best way to narrow the list might be to establish priorities. Here is how I would do it. I would start by prayerfully asking God to give you and the student wisdom as you consider how and where the student can become best equipped to be all God created him or her to be. There is nothing wrong with shooting high—no individual is insignificant. Everyone can make a difference and should want to.

Priority 1: Get the student's commitment to getting a good education.

Priority 2: Get the student to realize the importance of the peer group he or she will associate with in college and to commit to finding such a group no matter which college or university is chosen.

Priority 3: Identify colleges that have a strong sense of community and a 24/7 residential learning environment. I am convinced that a good residential college with a learning environment is an important stimulus to make the student learn and is better for most students than commuter colleges, where there are so many distractions beyond the control of the academic administrators.

Priority 4: Identify schools that will help the student be able to do more than make a living and that will help the student develop a deeper sense of meaning and purpose.

Priority 5: Identify colleges that will have a student body that will challenge but not overwhelm the student.

Priority 6: Identify colleges that have academic programs that meet the student's interest. Remember, however, that about half of all students interested in science change their minds in the first year and that most students change their declared major several times. Be sure there is a wide enough range of majors to choose from if the original choice turns out not to be the final choice.

Priority 7: Identify a range of schools in terms of cost, prestige, and selectivity. There should be some schools that the student may not get into and that you may not be able to afford without sufficient financial aid. There should also be some schools that you can be certain the student can get into and afford without a large financial-aid package.

Priority 8: Identify schools according to region of the country or type of campus (urban or rural, for example).

As you find colleges that interest you, call their admissions office and ask that they send you information. Most have an 800 number. Be prepared, however. Once you are on the list, you can expect to continue to receive information. Most people end up with a large box of college information.

Visit Colleges and Fill Out Applications

Once you have narrowed the list, you will want to visit the campuses during the student's junior year of high school. I would suggest taking off several days at a time, clustering colleges to visit geographically so that you can visit as many as possible in the least amount of time. It is probably unrealistic to consider visiting more than ten colleges.

On the initial visit, you may limit your visit to a half day, but be sure that you actually sit in classes. The college may want to control your visit, but you are in the driver's seat. Tell the college what you want to see and ask them to arrange it for you. If you are interested in particular programs such as music, sports, or a certain major, don't hesitate to ask to meet with professors in those areas. Most colleges will be happy to accommodate you if you give enough notice of your visit.

By the fall of the senior year, the student should know which schools he or she intends to apply to. It is best to apply by January 1, although most schools will accept applications until the school's financial-aid deadline, often March 1. Most schools have an application fee, but the real cost may be in terms of time. Filling out applications is a long but informative process. Though applications are ostensibly designed to help the college assess the student, you can tell a lot about the college by the information it asks for. Parents should read through the application. Be wary of applications that don't ask for enough information. Look at the essay questions. If there aren't any essay questions, that should raise questions. Also, the types of essay questions will tell you a lot about what is important to the school and the type of student it is looking for. Students should be prepared to spend a lot of time filling out applications. It is best to write the essays separately before using any forms supplied by the school.

Once the list has been narrowed to the student's top three choices, visit the schools again. This time, plan for the student to stay in a dorm. You will need to arrange this with the college, although not all colleges will encourage this. If it cannot be arranged through the college, perhaps the student can stay with a friend. I think a good visit starts with Thursday arrival near dinnertime, an evening in the dorm, going to three or four classes Friday morning, seeing other areas of interest Friday afternoon, and returning home Friday evening or Saturday morning. You may want to stay over until Sunday to go to a local church frequented by college students. Don't hesitate to ask the school to provide meal tickets while the student is on campus, because eating in the college dining hall can also be instructive. You may want to participate in some of the same activities, but not necessarily with the student. Trust your child to make good observations and have good judgment.

Apply for Financial Aid

For most students, the choices are now clear, and they usually know where they want to go. Now you must fill out the financial-aid applications. The process is much the same at all colleges that must meet federal guidelines. You will need the prior year's income tax forms.

(This is why you can't complete the process until the end of a calendar year. Schools will want the most recent calendar-year information.) You will also need to be ready to supply information concerning assets that may be available. Remember, the fundamental responsibility for a child's education is with the family—the federal financial-aid system seeks to ensure that parents do *all* they can possibly do. Most parents are not really prepared for the reordering of financial priorities that the government expects. So be ready to be surprised!

A few schools are so well endowed that they can be "need blind." That is, they will provide all the financial aid any student *needs* (not wants) to make the college acceptable. But most schools will prioritize applicants according to *need* or *merit* or a combination of the two. Need-based aid is aid awarded strictly on the basis of need. Some colleges, in order to get the most out of their financial aid, will start with low-need students and go toward the high-need students, but some colleges want economic diversity and will favor high-need students.

Merit-based aid is any aid that does not take need into account. It encompasses athletic scholarships, geographic scholarships, diversity scholarships, academic scholarships, and leadership scholarships. Often colleges receive large gifts that provide an annual scholarship to certain types of students, such as students interested in nursing or some particular major. All such aid is considered merit-based aid and is awarded to the most meritorious students, regardless of need.

Most schools combine need-based and merit-based awards. For instance, they may rank the students according to merit and then give need-based awards in addition to merit awards. Sometimes the system of awarding aid is so complicated that even those in the financial-aid office cannot predict who will get awards. This is why, however, it is important to meet the financial-aid deadlines, because few schools will make awards to students who apply after the deadline.

Students may also qualify for college-sponsored work-study positions. These are paying jobs on campus. The pay typically varies from job to job and from campus to campus, and it can go from minimum wage to more than ten dollars an hour. The hours worked may vary from five to fifteen hours a week.

In addition to awards by the institution, a student may be eligible for federal grants. These are normally available only to families in the lower-income brackets, depending on the number of children in a family.

Once all things have been considered, the college financial-aid office puts all of the awards together in the form of a financial-aid "package." If the package does not equal the "full cost" of attending the college (tuition, room, board, fees, and normal travel and miscellaneous expenses), the package will typically include loans. The loans may be federally subsidized or they may be loans that the family must make outside of the financial-aid system. It is worth noting that some families choose to make accelerated payments on their mortgage so that when college costs are expected to be high, the family can partially remortgage their home and still deduct the interest on loans that may have to be taken out. Other forms of interest are not deductible.

The government will require that the family provide money from any form of savings before the government will provide grants, and most colleges follow the same procedure.

Some students receive money from relatives, but designated gifts are not deductible as charitable deductions.

The issue of student loans is always a subject of many debates, for which there is no easy answer. But I will lay out the two sides of the debate.

In Favor of Student Loans

Taking loans increases a student's commitment to getting the most out of education. The student knows that he or she must repay the loan and that the education is costly. It is an unmotivated student who is unwilling to invest in his or her own self-improvement. And when you amortize the cost of college loans over the expected earnings increase over the life of the student, the cost is very small. For example, twenty thousand dollars' worth of loans is of little consequence when compared to extra income of ten thousand dollars a year for more than thirty years. In the long run, nothing is more worthy of investment than a good education.

In Opposition to Student Loans

Taking loans teaches a student to borrow without assets, to presume on the future. The inevitable result is that the student starts out life in debt and has fewer options in terms of career choice. The student *has* to find a high-paying job. Before the student even starts a career, he or she has fallen into the American debt trap of running faster and faster just to keep up. It is better to learn to live within your means.

You need to help your student make a principled decision regarding the cost of education. I am convinced that too many people make the decision prematurely. After financial-aid awards, the apparent disparity in cost between different colleges is often far less than anticipated.

Every college can tell you that they have students attending from every financial-aid bracket. Covenant always has some students whose family income is below the total cost of attendance. Some of the most rewarding moments of being a college president is seeing students overcome financial adversity, apply themselves to their studies, graduate, get good jobs, and promptly pay off their loans. I'm convinced that such students often get more out of college than those who had no financial need to overcome.

Parents need to realize that adversity is not to be feared and to encourage their students to incur the cost (I'm talking about much more than financial cost) of getting a good education.

6

What Students Need from a College Education

Too many parents seem to lump all colleges together. In other words, they assume that since you get the same degree (a B.A. or a B.S.), you get the same education. But it is important to realize that curriculum varies tremendously from college to college.

Understanding the College Curriculum

Every college has a catalog that describes all the course offerings as well as the graduation requirements. The word used for the courses required to graduate is "curriculum." Curriculum consists of general education courses, distribution courses, electives, and major fields of study.

Courses are given numbers. Usually courses beginning with the number one are primarily for freshmen, courses beginning with two are for sophomores, etc. So a three-hundred-level course is considered a junior-level course.

The university might have a College of Arts and Sciences, a Law School, and a Medical School. The College of Arts and Sciences is made up of different academic departments such as Math, English, History, Biology, Chemistry, Music, Political Science, Philosophy and Religion, etc.

Most colleges require that students major in a field of study described in the college catalog. Normally, from one-third to one-half of the total college credit hours are taken in the major field of study. The rest of the courses are taken either as electives or as general education courses consisting of required or distribution courses. Usually, each department has broad latitude in deciding what courses are required for a major. Some departments require as few as thirty credit hours of three-hundred- and four-hundred-level courses, while other majors may require as much as fifty or sixty credit hours. Sometimes graduation requirements, especially major requirements, make it difficult, if not impossible, for a student to complete college in four years. Parents need to pay attention, because this can be an unexpected and costly surprise to learn in the fourth year that a fifth year of college will be required for the student to graduate.

Usually, a degree requires approximately 120 semester credit hours. (An hour is usually fifty minutes at most colleges.) A credit hour is defined as one classroom hour per week for a whole semester, which typically consists of approximately sixteen weeks. A three-credit course has three fifty-minute classes each week. Most students take an average of five three-credit-hour courses each semester for a total of fifteen credit hours a semester, thirty credit hours a year. A student taking fifteen hours should be in class fifteen hours a week, not counting labs. A three-hour lab may only count for one credit hour since the lab may require little or no homework. A student is supposed to study two hours out of class for every hour in class, so a student who is in class fifteen hours and studies thirty hours has a forty-five-hour week.

Students are evaluated in each course, with an A being equal to a 4, a B equal to a 3, etc. Students who fail to attain a 2.0 grade point average cannot graduate. The grade and the credit hours are combined and a weighted grade point average (GPA) is calculated at the end of each semester. So, a student with a 3.2 GPA has more credit hours with a B than with an A. A 4.0 GPA means the student made all A's.

Coming into education from a nonacademic background, I was surprised by the general "faith" that a college degree means something. I intentionally use the word "faith" to emphasize both the depth and unquestioning nature of this belief. The "faith" in the system is faith that graduates who earn a degree have been well educated. What makes this faith so remarkable is that there is so much variation in what goes into a degree. Differences exist between a large research university and a small liberal arts college, between residential colleges and commuter colleges, between Internet courses and courses taught in the classroom with a professor, between lecture courses and seminars. And this is only the beginning. There are different levels of rigor, different competitive environments, different abilities of the students, and different levels of involvement in the learning process.

The common denominator ends up being faith that faculty members put together worthwhile courses and accurately evaluate students' mastery of the subject matter. However, even methods of evaluation vary widely within the same department of the same school. The point is that we place great faith in the faculty, but is this faith warranted by the training the faculty has received? It is worth noting that the breadth of education in the United States is greater than in most countries where the higher education system is much more uniform.

Most faculty members have spent years earning a Ph.D. in an academic discipline such as biology. He or she is very much aware of how much there is to learn. With the growth in knowledge in the modern world, majors develop specialty areas such as environmental biology rather than general biology. Even a person with a Ph.D. cannot begin to know the entire discipline. Professors are very much aware that they know only part of their own discipline; therefore, it is not surprising that faculty hold great respect for the knowledge that their colleagues have. A biology professor is not going to challenge an English professor regarding modern literature. An education professor is not going to correct a business professor's understanding of management.

Professors are not really experts in curriculum design; therefore they are reluctant to try to design a curriculum because they are not experts in that field. Yet they must approve changes in a curriculum. I think that this is why there is so much faith in the existing system. It must work; after all, it worked for them. In other words, the typical faculty member's primary concern is to teach the subject matter he or she knows well, not to design a curriculum for a student whom he or she does not know personally. Each faculty member assumes it is someone else's job to think about educating the whole student.

Now in one sense it is true that no matter what you study in college, it is of some value. Knowledge is always to be preferred over ignorance, and whenever educators are successful in reducing the level of ignorance among eighteen- to twenty-two-year-olds, they should take some satisfaction in that accomplishment. But continuing to offer education as it has been offered, especially considering how both the culture and students have changed, is worthy of scrutiny.

Major Fields of Study

The idea of majors seems to be based on the premise that each student needs to learn the foundations of at least one area of study. A college typically divides its majors into departments such as natural science, social science, humanities, and professional studies (business, education, computer science, etc.). Most students know that they must major in something in college; but the minority of these students comes to college knowing what their major will be. Those who think they know often change their minds two or three times. Once they graduate, many students' careers do not coincide with their choice of major.

No undergraduate major really prepares a person for a job; the place of employment typically trains new personnel to do what is required. (For example, a student who studies banking will typically not know how to do an entry-level job at a bank. The bank will train the individual to do that job.) It is important to recognize that a major requiring thirty-nine hours only consists of thirteen semester-long courses, hardly enough to master a discipline.

Nevertheless, there is value in beginning to approach a discipline systematically. In taking foundational courses, students begin to develop a framework for approaching a particular discipline. They learn that each discipline has a specialized vocabulary. They learn that each discipline has different methods of research and study that are unique to that discipline. If students graduate without knowing the "tools of the trade," they will not find entry into the trade easy.

It is also important to understand the terms and the methods of analysis of a given field; it is even more important to understand that other fields have different terms and methods of analysis. Students should be able to connect what they are learning in other departments with their major field of study. What should be learned is the interrelatedness of all knowledge and the complexities of any one field of study.

However, in the "cafeteria education" that has evolved, students are often unaware of the major divisions such as natural science, social science, humanities, etc., and do not see their interrelatedness. Graduates of the same institution do not possess a common set of skills, knowledge, and values. It is not unusual to find college graduates who cannot write well, do not know American history, have no knowledge of Western culture, or cannot do college algebra.

With such "diversity" of choice, universities have become multiversities. And if these kinds of differences exist in the curriculum, there is even less of a guarantee that graduates will have developed foundational skills, knowledge, and values. Students need to be forced to think about what it means to be a human being—not a pleasure-seeking being, not a productive being, not a sexual being, not a thinking being, not an emotional being—but a human being, with all that the words "human being" entail. Taking a concentration of courses in marketing, modern literature, marine biology, etc. does not necessarily help the student become a well-rounded human being.

The Importance of the College Environment

Too many students go to college ill-prepared academically, socially, mentally, or spiritually. There are millions of Americans who started but never completed college. The dropout rate is high (the national freshman dropout rate exceeds 20 percent). And this is not because students are unable to do the work. Colleges try to admit those capable of succeeding at the college or university level. They are able to assess the student's *potential* to succeed, but they cannot easily assess a student's *will* to succeed.

This is why the environment of the college is so important. The environment may be shaped primarily by extracurricular activities or it may be shaped by cocurricular activities that encourage and support the student who does not yet have good study skills, who is not highly motivated, who does not know what he or she wants to do, and who has never been a "good student" or one who loves to learn. Part of the college's job is to introduce students to a world they have never seen and get them excited to learn more about that world.

But an individual professor is often competing with the tug of another world the student has never seen— the world of independence. Particularly vulnerable to this world are those students whose greatest need is acceptance by others. We all need friends, but students who feel "lost" because their high school friends are no longer around have a very strong need to find new friends. And all too often the basis of such friendships has little to do with the purpose of college. If the friends they make don't like going to class and don't study, there are plenty of other enjoyable things to do.

But the *intentional* student will find other students who want to take advantage of the college experience. He or she will be intentional in choosing friends, and after a good education, this is the most important thing that is gained from going to college. The intentional student knows that college is a once-in-a-lifetime opportunity—not just an opportunity to make new friends and do whatever he or she wants—but an opportunity to learn new things that will make him or her into a new and better person. The intentional student won't want to miss such an opportunity. Let's explore these new things that transform the student.

Knowledge, Skills, and Values

I have found it helpful to divide what we learn into three somewhat arbitrary categories: knowledge, skills, and values. To illustrate the difference, I will use someone with whom most of us have experience—a medical doctor—and a common procedure—an appendectomy.

To be a doctor, one must acquire certain *knowledge*, such as biology, chemistry, and anatomy. In order to know whether to and how to remove an infected appendix, the doctor must know what an appendix is, how it is cut out, and what will happen if it is not removed.

But knowledge is not enough; the doctor must also develop certain *skills*. He or she must have diagnostic skills to be able to recognize the symptoms that would indicate a ruptured appendix. The doctor must have manual skills to be able to wield a scalpel, open the abdomen, remove the infected appendix, and close the incision without causing excessive bleeding, heart or lung failure, and infection. The doctor also must have people skills to be able to work with the patient and with other professionals, nurses, anesthesiologists, and support staff.

But knowledge and skills are not enough. The doctor must possess certain *values*. He or she must value human life and serving others more than his or her own time. He or she must not remove an appendix carelessly or needlessly, just to make money. The doctor may be called upon to make critical value judgments, such as how clear the evidence is that the appendix is infected and what is the potential for serious disability or death due to other medical conditions the patient may have. The doctor will even have to make value judgments concerning how he or she will use the money he or she makes or what to do when someone is sick and does not have insurance.

Using these three categories, knowledge, skills, and values, I would like to describe what I hope students learn in college.

We Are Made in the Creator's Image

If you think of people who are functional (or capable) and contrast them with people who are dysfunctional (or incapable), I would suggest that functional people have three important characteristics.

1. They have a sense of *purpose.*
2. They feel what they are doing is worth doing. They have a sense of *worth.*
3. They feel they are *capable* of doing what they are doing.

We want to be functional because God made us this way—he made each person to *exercise dominion.* Have you ever known someone who did not want to have control over his or her life? No one has control over all of life, but we do have areas of control—our desk, our home, our clothes. And we want to have control over our work. We want to be able to do it without someone looking over our shoulder all the time. This is why we are happiest when we know (1) what we are supposed to be doing, (2) that we are capable of doing that thing, and (3) that it is worth doing. This is true for the simple things of life such as balancing your checkbook, driving a car, or knitting a scarf, but it also pertains to your primary vocation. God literally made us to do "good works" that he prepared before the beginning of time.

Part of exercising dominion is creating—making or doing something new. We are made in the Creator's image—we are made to create. I know that most people don't consider themselves "creative," but every time you fix a meal, solve a problem, or go to a new place, you are being creative. You are doing something that you have never done before. Each day is a new day, unlike any other day. Whether it is the detour on the way to work, a disgruntled coworker, or a new customer, you are going to be facing new situations that will require creative solutions.

I would argue that colleges should be helping students develop the knowledge, skills, and values to make important connections so that they can be creative and exercise dominion over what God has entrusted to them. I am a strong advocate of the value of a liberal arts education that helps the individual make important connections that will enhance his or her ability to exercise dominion creatively.[1] As unconnected individuals, we are literally just specks on the planet. If you are without the ability to make connections, you could picture yourself this way.

.

If you look closely, you will see a dot between the last sentence and this sentence. Too many people see themselves this way. They see themselves as living an insignificant life, as someone who would never be missed, as doing something anyone could do.

But a college education should help the student make connections to all of life in the following ways:

1. Learning how to communicate orally, in writing, and with numbers helps us connect to others.
2. Learning how to communicate nonverbally through art and music helps us connect with others who may not share our language or background.
3. Learning where we are in the history of ideas helps us connect with the past so that we can learn from those who preceded us.
4. Learning how the physical world works helps us recognize that we are also physical beings and helps us connect to the physical world around us.
5. Learning how the social world works helps us connect to families, communities, churches, and governments that are so important in all our lives.
6. Learning that the human body requires proper nourishment and exercise and that it ages and passes through various stages enables us to get the most life out of our bodies.
7. Learning that life, as we know it, is brief helps us connect with the ultimate meaning and purpose of life.

Suddenly the student's world is transformed. He or she is now in the center of life and loves it! There is joy in discovery, in seeking new solutions, in being a part of the solution and not part of the problem. The student is not fearful of life slipping by. The student knows that life has different stages and wants to drink richly from the wellspring of life that he or she is in.

All individuals are small, but when they are connected to a bigger world, an exciting world, and a world that needs them, they find a world of ultimate purpose and

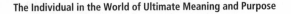

The Individual in the World of Ultimate Meaning and Purpose

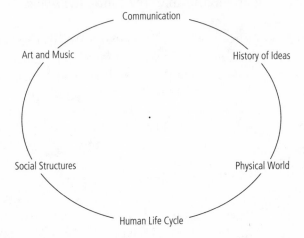

meaning because it has the potential of being the beginning of eternal life with the Creator.

I would like to add two caveats. The first is that no matter how much we are able to make these important connections, we must recognize that our knowledge and our perspective are very limited. We never really have sufficient information to have total dominion. There are always new ways of looking at things, new ways to be creative. To put this another way, we never have all the information to give us complete control; that would make us God. A good education, however, makes us appropriately hesitant, humble, and willing to consider other points of view.

The second caveat is a corollary of the first; just because our knowledge and perspective are limited is no excuse for not taking the risk of exercising dominion or being creative. A good education prepares us to consider as many sources of disparate information as possible and to synthesize that information into a coherent concept so that we can appropriately act. In short, a good education helps us avoid the paralysis of overanalysis.

To illustrate the importance of making connections, consider again a patient with an infected appendix.

> The patient is from a foreign country and speaks a language the doctor does not speak, so that the doctor is unable to ask the patient important diagnostic questions.
>
> The doctor is able to show the patient pictures that will enable the patient to know what must be done.
>
> The patient is poor and uneducated and has never been in a hospital.
>
> The patient is overweight, a heavy smoker, and in poor physical health.
>
> The patient has no family or friends present and is apparently in her seventies.
>
> The patient is an animist who appears to believe in evil spirits and feels under the attack of an evil spirit.

As you can see, the doctor who wants to exercise dominion in this case has to make a lot of important connections in a very creative way. Unless the doctor is able to make all the important connections, he may be unable to save the patient, even though he has the skill and knowledge necessary to remove the appendix.

Analytical Skills and Communication

A further aspect of being made as human beings created in the image of God is that humans possess the ability to think creatively, to analyze, and to communicate. Critical thinking requires appropriate gathering of information and making sense out of it. If two people are given the same information, it is possible for one person to draw correct conclusions and the other person to draw incorrect conclusions. "Critical thinking is, in short, self-directed, self-disciplined, self-monitored, and self-corrected thinking. It presupposes assent to rigorous standards of excellence and mindful command of their use. It entails effective communication and problem-solving abilities and a commitment to overcome our nation's egocentrism and sociocentrism."[2]

Few schools require logic courses of all students; however, a good exam may test both a person's logical capacity and analytical capacity. Perhaps the first and most important step in developing a good judgment is analyzing the problem correctly. Often people solve a problem only to find that the apparent problem was not the real problem. Subject matter exams that require the student to write an essay test the ability of the student to identify the important issues and analyze them. Professors who know a subject well can quickly determine if the student has analyzed the subject correctly.

Once a concept is grasped, the human response is to communicate the findings. Whether this communication is done in the form of a musical piece, a scientific paper, a rhetorical argument, or a poem is not important. What is important is that we are able to share what we have learned with others. The Greeks felt that the human ability to reason and to communicate separates us from all other forms of life in creation. Certainly, few skills are more important than communication skills. For instance, when students graduate from college without knowing the basic rules of grammar and punctuation, they are severely disadvantaged. When students know something but are unable to effectively present it to others, they are severely disadvantaged.

Part of good communication also requires the ability to relate. Aristotle felt that to be persuasive, the audience must feel the speaker is virtuous. If the person receiving the message does not trust the one speaking, the argument may fall on deaf ears. Communication skills are developed not only in the classroom but also in interaction among peers. A college needs to educate students in such a way that students hold each other accountable to speak and write cogently and truthfully.

Learning to Make Wise Choices

While the distinction between knowledge, skills, and values is admittedly somewhat arbitrary and simplistic, it illustrates just how complicated the learning process is. While it is evident that we all need knowledge, skills, and values to do any task, I would argue that what we expect most from those in positions of responsibility is good judgment. We want others to have common sense, which seems not so common these days.

When we observe the world around us and analyze it, we are forced to make some judgment concerning what we have seen. And good judgment is the wisdom to know what to do in a given situation. I think that good judgment has always been hard to develop, but it has never been more important than it is now, because the world in which we live is so interconnected.

For example, a doctor cannot rest on what he has learned. He must stay in touch with teaching organizations in order to stay current in his field. He must operate within a health-care system that is a blend of public, private, and medical systems. He must work with other health-care professionals to help provide the best treatments. Since he must depend on other trained health-care professionals, he must be supportive of their training and willing to pay for their services.

A doctor is a part of other complex, interconnected systems. He relies on electricity, heating and air conditioning, sterile instruments, medicines, available operating rooms, ambulance services, reliable vehicles, high-ways, police, and paramedics.

And doing the surgery is just the beginning. A doctor must know how to build a practice, to use Medicare and Medicaid, to train receptionists and housekeepers, to rent office space. Once he gets paid, he must understand enough of the economy to make wise investments so he can send his children to school and have enough for retirement. And he must understand enough about education to help his children make wise choices.

In short, all of us are constantly being called on to render good judgments, and the judgments we make are multifaceted decisions that require us to use a broad array of skills and knowledge. However, many of the judgments we make will be outside of our specific training, so we must learn how and when to trust others.

Conclusion

Two researchers, Pascarella and Terenzini, authors of *How College Affects Students*, concluded that college makes a difference in learning power, values, and prin-cipled moral reasoning. The effect appears to be great-est in four-year, residential colleges where students are *involved* in college life. And the effects of college are life-long and transgenerational (affecting children of col-lege graduates).

College graduates as a whole have greater ability to reason abstractly, greater skill in using reason and evi-dence to address issues, and greater intellectual flexi-bility to see strengths and weaknesses in different sides of a complex issue. College students manifest an increase in moral and religious values, moving from constraint to individual freedom, from narrowness to breadth, from exclusiveness to inclusiveness, from simplicity to complexity, and from intolerance to tolerance.

Finally, Pascarella and Terenzini concluded that college graduates experience higher earnings, more stable employment, higher levels of career mobility, and better health. They make wiser consumer choices, save more, and are more effective in using discretionary sources for long-term investment.[3]

But are we looking at all the evidence and making all the connections we should make before concluding that colleges are doing a good job? Here are the things that worry me.

1. Half of the students who enter college do not graduate in six years. It is well known that the quality of education varies widely not only between students of different colleges but also between students within a particular college. This is a major warning signal that something may be wrong.
2. The United States is the wealthiest and most educated country in the world. Why then is it a country marked by so much family breakdown, illiteracy, crime, poverty, and drug abuse? One out of five adults over twenty-five is a college graduate, and it is the college graduates who hold most of the leadership positions in society. College graduates are our lawyers and physicians, and our business, education, and government leaders. They produce the television shows and movies; they lead in art and entertainment. If college is doing such a good job, why are the graduates so ill-prepared to tackle the questions that threaten us all?

Cynics, and there are many today, would say that what colleges really teach is anything but helpful. Bad teachers are tolerated, even protected. Colleges use their best faculty to make the college known, but once students are enrolled, they are taught by graduate assistants with no reputation and little experience. Lax standards allow students to do sloppy work, turn it in late, and still get passing grades. Students learn to fake it, to postpone it, to lie about it, to do whatever it takes to get a grade. All of this leads to students who value material gain above all else, who are not prepared to do quality work.

Other critics would say that political correctness, tolerance, and the importance of feeling good about oneself have disabled rather than enabled students who no longer know how to make important qualitative distinctions. Getting a degree from a well-known school is more important than working to correct the ills of society.

The premise of this chapter is that parents and their children benefit most when they think more about what they want and expect out of a college education. If students make their college decision on the basis of friends, location, and cost rather than on the curriculum, can we be surprised if they do not get a good education, especially one that will benefit society at large?

In a free-market society, colleges are heavily influenced by the desires of the market. But this does not relieve the individual college of the responsibility to carefully consider the needs of students and to meet those needs, even if prospective students may not immediately be attracted. Just as the doctor may prescribe a medical solution that the patient would prefer to avoid, the college must be willing to prescribe an educational solution that may be painful but beneficial.

7

Why Colleges Fail
to Give Students
What They Need

It seems obvious that students change from generation to generation and that colleges should modify the curriculum, not to respond to the desires of students but to meet their needs. Is there evidence that colleges are not meeting these needs? I would like to cite five reasons why I don't think colleges are meeting students' needs.

The first reason is that there is great dismay among employers concerning the ability of college graduates. In recent years there has been a national trend to require colleges to assess how well they are doing what they say they are doing. The demand for assessment emerges from the dissatisfaction of taxpayers with the higher education establishment and the students they are graduating.

The second reason is that students are detached from the academic process. A learning environment does exist in some colleges (not necessarily just the prestigious colleges), but it does not exist in most colleges. For too many students, learning is of secondary importance. Friends, infotainment, parties, sex, or work often consume students' time and interest; learning is a necessary nuisance. We tend to excuse this as nothing more than youthful exuberance. Sure, it is hard to get students interested in school, but we cannot accept the "before five" and "after five" cultures.

The third reason is that most students do not finish the college they started. Those who claim that ease of access into college is what causes the problem have not talked to students. Students are not dropping out because college is too hard. They are dropping out because they do not study, are not willing to sacrifice financially, have no career plans, are not sure why they are in college, and do not see the relevance of their courses.

The fourth reason is the destructive lifestyle that dominates American campuses. Excessive drinking is the most obvious social problem on most campuses, but obsession with sex is easily the most serious problem, which has long-lasting consequences. The promiscuous party atmosphere that pervades college life speaks loudly and clearly to the fact that many students are not seriously engaged in the learning process.

The fifth reason is found in society itself. We have to ask whether societal leaders learned what they should have in college when society is known for family breakdown, drug abuse, promiscuous sex, and crime. To say that such signs of moral decadence are a result of our wealth is to suggest that the solution is to become poor. How ridiculous! I once asked a student who had taken a course on the family at a secular university what she was learning. She talked about the changing nature of the family, two-working-parent families, flex hours, etc. When I asked if the "new" family was better than the old, she said they never talked about that. When I asked if the class discussed how to build strong families, she said no. Something is wrong with such an education.

But, unfortunately, there are many impediments to changing higher education. Let's consider some of these impediments.

Cultural Impediments

Educators assume that students come from families and churches that provide the foundation for meaning and purpose, and that this is not the role of the college. This mind-set says that colleges can only be held responsible for teaching those things that can be known through research and analysis. Values are personal; each person reaches his or her own conclusion about what is important.

In the sixties, frustrated college administrators, unable to control students, decided that colleges could no longer act *in loco parentis* (in place of the parents). So college students were declared adults. Colleges collectively washed their hands of the responsibility of trying to enforce lifestyle behavior and withdrew to requiring students to meet only academic requirements. Thus, most colleges no longer concern themselves with values.

And, in addition, as society has become more culturally and religiously diverse, the Judeo-Christian foundation of Western society has come under intense scrutiny, even attack. The old core courses, such as Western civilization, assumed students would arrive at class with a Judeo-Christian worldview and reinforced this view. But new courses attempt to show the many diverse cultures that shape our culture, including the African-American influence, the Native-American influence, and the more recent Asian and Hispanic influence. There has also been a trend to teach multiculturalism and feminism as modern cultural concepts.

Market forces have influenced colleges, especially the drive for global economic hegemony, and colleges have responded to the drive for economic success following World War II. Soft courses in religion and philosophy are considered less important than practical studies in business, science, social science, and engineering.

As a college president, I must ask, "Are we giving students what they need? Or are we giving what the students want?" Certainly, parents of elementary and high school students expect educators to ask this question. I am convinced that even parents of college-age students expect me to ask this question. It is reprehensible when colleges pander to students by giving them what they want (rather than what they need) primarily for the purpose of attracting them to the school.

Organizational Impediments

The faculty of modern colleges is far more diverse and has difficulty dealing as a body with the subject of meaning and purpose. Surveys have shown that faculty members are less likely to be religious than the general population. In fact, many faculty members are openly resistant to the inclusion of any religious perspectives in the shaping of the academic enterprise. And those who are religious often hold such diverse religious views that consensus is difficult to attain. In general, college educators are more likely to see objective analysis as more important than religious conviction, which represents uninformed bias. It is politically easier to replace these core courses with distribution courses. Even at a Christ-centered college like Covenant, the process of changing the core takes years.

Many of the colleges started after World War II did not even begin with a strong core curriculum. From the beginning, these universities were formed to meet the need for a trained workforce, and the schools did not have the moral or ethical commitment that is essential to form a community. Colleges became places for individual faculty members to work rather than learning communities. Increased specialization caused individual faculty members to give up responsibility for the whole education of the whole student.

In addition, traditional faculty absented itself from moral or personal matters and turned this responsibility over to trained professionals who usually serve under administrators other than the chief academic officer. Health services treat and counsel sexually active students. Psychological counselors help students who drink too much or who suffer from depression or anorexia. The student development department offers "college life" courses dealing with time management, study skills, homesickness, etc. Career counseling helps students learn their aptitudes and choose majors. The financial-aid department helps students struggling to pay for college.

The role of the president has also changed considerably. With larger colleges and with competition for students and financial resources, the responsibilities of running colleges are so great that presidents have become primarily revenue producers. Most presidents are so involved in influencing state appropriations or winning the support of other potential funding agents that they have little to do with the educational philosophy of the college. They are judged on the basis of a balanced budget and a growing college, not on the basis of the philosophy of education. Quality education is synonymous with resources—successful fund-raising, large libraries, well-paid faculty, large research grants. Without strong administrative leadership, it is easy for the self-interest of professors to inform decisions rather than what is in the student's best interest.

The average tenure of a college president is about six or seven years. Many faculty members have the attitude that if they don't like the president's initiatives, all that is necessary is to wait until the president leaves and a new president arrives. Because changing a college core is so difficult, a president would be foolish to initiate the process without the strong support of the board.

But even the board seems powerless. I once was talking to the chairman of the board of a prestigious private college about the matters discussed in this book. He professed to be a Christian and acknowledged concern for the matter of character development of students. This man was enormously wealthy, one of the largest donors to the university, and he had been very successful in getting others to give to the university. He also had a close relationship with the president, a man who was very secure in his position, with an enviable record of accomplishment. The chairman asked what I would suggest for character development. I recommended that the university require all students to study the most widely read and influential book in Western civilization. He immediately knew what I was saying. "We could never get the faculty to go along with requiring students to read the Bible," he said.

Colleges, especially large universities, are known to be virtually ungovernable. The former governor of Tennessee, Lamar Alexander, became president of the University of Tennessee, and when he left that job to become the United States Secretary of Education, the joke was that he left being president of the university because the job was too political.

Faculty Impediments

To earn a doctorate, a faculty member had to do original research. With thousands of doctoral candidates doing their theses each year, an earned doctorate increasingly means that the college professor is a specialist in a very narrow field. Many professors do not possess a broad perspective and fail to see the advantage of it.

Once a professor starts at a university, he or she wants to earn tenure. Tenure is a matter of both job security and prestige. It is granted after approximately seven years, but it is not granted in all cases. At many large universities, tenure is granted because of the research and publishing that the professor has done. Many professors went into education out of love for the discipline and the desire to continue their study of it. With the added incentive of tenure, faculty members are not likely to be as concerned with the education of the whole student as are professors who go into teaching to mold and shape students.

Teaching is a profession, an honorable one, in which individuals are more or less self-employed. There are many reasons people choose a career in education, but undoubtedly one of the reasons is to be a professional person with little competition or accountability. This type of teacher does not feel the need to be held accountable, because he or she is intrinsically motivated. Therefore, teachers are reluctant to accept accountability for the outcome of students—especially outcomes for which they feel little responsibility. Professors hold one another accountable, through various faculty committees, in matters related to provision of quality academic content. But this seldom addresses the area of values.

For reasons that are unclear to me, college professors are among the least religious of all groups in America.

Many of them search for meaning and purpose in the pursuit of knowledge rather than religious truth. And while professors may accept those who teach about religions, they are suspicious of anyone, even if he or she has academic credentials, who teaches as a believer in the religion. Professors are supposed to be impassioned advocates, people who have something to profess, but what professors profess today is empirical knowledge gained as a result of their study and research, devoid of values. They are certainly not to profess religious beliefs, which are considered personal and irrelevant to the discipline. They believe that they must be objective and that religion is inherently subjective.[1] Lack of personal faith combined with suspicion of relating faith to knowledge makes it almost impossible for a professor to educate the sum of the mental, emotional, physical, and spiritual aspects of a person. Teachers are often dysfunctional outside of their field of research and find themselves incapable of teaching "the whole person." To even suggest such a responsibility is threatening to teachers' concept of their role.

Assessment Impediments

As a concept, assessment is in vogue in higher education. The concept is simple: Colleges establish learning goals and determine how well students are progressing toward those goals. When areas of weakness are identified, corrective measures need to be taken; new goals must be established so there is continual improvement of the educational outcome.

Assessment is just a tool. It is not a substitute for true leadership. Assessment can easily become merely another bureaucratic system in colleges that already have many layers of bureaucracy.

Assessment is currently used as a reason why general goals, such as providing a sense of meaning and purpose, should not be implemented. Assessment implies having goals that are realistic, achievable, and measurable. Some of the most important outcomes of college are difficult to assess. The president of a Christian college told me that rather than have non-Christians assess a goal such as teaching students to serve, his college simply took the goal out of the college's purpose statement. (When a college is reaccredited, a peer-review team comes in to assure that the college is meeting its stated purpose. Since most colleges are secular, the likely composition of the team is non-Christian.)

Just because something is difficult to assess does not mean that it can't be assessed or that it should not be a goal. Let me suggest some potential objectives.

The core curriculum must consist of 25 percent of the graduation requirement and include courses that address the essential issues of the meaning and purpose of life. No course should be excluded because it teaches a particular religious perspective (Judaism, Christianity, Islam, etc.). The committee that designs the core must have representation from the following divisions of the college: languages (including English), art and music, philosophy and literature, social sciences, natural sciences, physical education, and religion.

Seventy-five percent of the students should graduate from this college within six years (assuming that it is possible for the typical student to graduate in four years).

The college will provide credit-bearing opportunities for students to experience other cultures and make such opportunities a graduation requirement.

The college will provide credit-bearing opportunities for students to gain work experience related to the academic enterprise.

Even though it is possible to have an objective of trying to help students develop a sense of meaning and purpose and to assess the results, assessment is a distraction that enables colleges to have very easily attainable and measurable (albeit less important) objectives.

Conclusion

The goal of education must be clear: to get students actively involved in a community of learning with a strong core curriculum that addresses the real needs of the modern American student. The value of the process to create such an environment must be reiterated over and over again. It is the role of the faculty, not the student, to dictate what every student needs to know. To abrogate this responsibility is to admit that colleges are like ships without a rudder.

I am not advocating, as have others, merely a return to the past, where the core attempted to inculcate in students the core values of Western civilization. While I support such efforts, I don't think they go far enough, because they do not address the issue of meaning and purpose. The old cores were built for a different generation of students. To reach today's student, colleges must have a different starting point.

A Curriculum
That Develops
Knowledgeable Faith

Nothing more clearly demonstrates why many colleges fail to give students what they need more than the lack of knowledge concerning religion. Students used to go to college to develop a meaningful philosophy of life. Now they go to college mainly to be well-off financially (see the following chart). As has been argued, many forces have been at work to bring us to this point, but schools fail students when they do not require students to develop an overall philosophy of life that gives a transcendent source of meaning and purpose.

Life Goals of College Freshmen

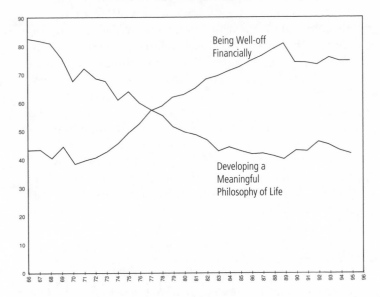

The Search for Meaning and Purpose

The search for meaning and purpose is not new. Education has a rich tradition of helping students find meaningful answers to the all-important questions. For centuries, students gained insight through the study of history, art, science, religion, philosophy, and literature. The great mistake that we make today, however, is that we want to expose students to a lot of information without helping them know how to evaluate that information. There seems to be a fear of indoctrinating students, and this fear leads us to the other extreme—we acquaint but we do not inform.

Consider the following excerpt from noted Princeton sociologist Robert Wuthnow:

During the 1960s a sharp liberalization of attitudes also took place in a wide variety of lifestyle issues, ranging

114

from divorce and premarital sex to political and economic orientations. . . . Virtually every study, moreover, showed that the growing liberalization of American culture in these years was closely related to the rising influence of higher education. Some of the influence seemed directly attributable to the ideas that were being taught, for example, greater awareness of crosscultural guarantees of civil liberties and deeper understanding of the relativity of cultural preferences. The remainder seemed more from indirect sources—from the circuitous influence of more liberal elites in politics, the mass media and entertainment industry—and simply from the diversifying influences of living away from parents on college campuses amidst the turmoil and experimentation of the period.

In any case, the influences of higher education were sufficiently direct for polls and surveys generally to find differences in levels of education to be the single best predictor of differences in attitudes and values. . . . The better educated tended to be more liberal on a wide variety of issues. . . . Participation in conventional kinds of religious activities began to slip noticeably among the better educated. Consequently, there was a considerable "education gap" in religious commitment by the end of the 1960s.[1]

As the president of a Christ-centered college, I saw Christian students who come in and think they have all the answers concerning their faith. As they take six hours of required Bible and six more hours of required Christian doctrine, I see the good effects of learning systematically about one's faith. But this does not mean that they accept all that their teachers believe, nor does it mean that they are uninterested in other religions and philosophies.

Neither does it mean that study of one's faith makes one have less faith. Many seem to believe that faith and learning are opposites, but nothing could be farther from the truth. Faith is a product of learning. Without learning, religious conviction tends to be superstitious, dogmatic, and bigoted.

Colleges are now so big and so numerous that they could easily require religious study and offer options to students of various religious backgrounds. Most people in this country are Christian, but there is no reason why large universities could not teach the basic tenets of Judaism, Islam, and Hinduism to students from those religious backgrounds.

More than 85 percent of all entering students claim to believe in God, but for those who prefer a philosophical approach, they could learn how various philosophies approach the subject of meaning and purpose without the necessity of a divine being.

Students are not dumb. They want to know the answers to the most important questions in life. Why are we here? Where are we going? Because of the fear of offending people, however, colleges have increasingly avoided matters of faith. George Marsden, author of *The Soul of the American University*, concludes that the one thing that cannot be discussed on most campuses is personal faith.[2] This is in spite of the distinctly religious nature of our population and history of our colleges.

In an interview regarding his new book, *The People's Religion: American Faith in the 90's*, noted pollster George Gallup was quoted as saying, "Over the last 54 years of scientific polling, religion in America has been remarkably stable." He went on to say, however,

> Many are just putting a religion together that is comfortable for them and is not necessarily challenging. Somebody called it religion à la carte. That's the central weakness of Christianity in this country today: There is not a sturdiness of belief. There is a lack of knowledge

of Christianity, a lack of awareness of Christian doctrines of atonement, redemption, and grace. Many Americans don't have a grasp of these things, and yet eight out of ten say they are Christians.[3]

With less than half the population regularly attending church and with many immigrants coming from other religions, more and more people are being swept up by everything from Satan worship to the current New Age rage.

Ignorance in matters of faith is as serious, if not more serious, than ignorance in other areas. College students would be well served if they were forced to be self-conscious about such matters. My experience is that most students are more than willing to express their convictions, but they are almost oblivious to their ignorance concerning their religious beliefs.

Expected Benefits

If colleges were to require students to take courses whose primary purpose is to teach a particular religious perspective on the meaning and purpose of life, colleges would have to ensure that students were taught by competent advocates of that position who were also knowledgeable about other religious and philosophical systems. But to avoid education that is really indoctrination, students would need to develop the tools to evaluate what they are being taught.

This means that educators would have to teach students how to validate what they believe. And there are three ways people validate what they say they believe. (1) It has to be rational or logical. (2) It has to work. (3) It has to be grounded in some transcendent or external reality, some system bigger than ourselves.

Therefore, one of the major benefits of helping students develop a sense of meaning and purpose is that it also requires colleges to teach students how to analyze and how to think, especially conceptually. The study of religion and philosophy forces students to think more conceptually, more deeply, more critically, and more logically than the study of more concrete subjects.

Though the Hindus believe that all roads lead to God, I do not. There are real differences in various religious perspectives. But one thing does seem to be true: Students who are religious are more likely to have a personal sense of purpose and be more interested in serving others. If students were self-consciously aware of what they profess to believe, I think they would more readily desire to develop their capabilities so that they could engage in worthwhile work. The person who has a higher purpose for living is more likely to see the relevance of work to that purpose. And so we work for a higher purpose, one that is closely aligned with our deepest beliefs.

When a person wants to do meaningful work, he or she then wants to develop the capabilities necessary to do that work. What I am saying is that students with a clear sense of meaning and purpose are more likely to see the value of a vocation and, therefore, more likely to be interested in taking courses that enable them to successfully pursue that vocation.

As a Christian, I strongly believe in the presence of evil in this world, and I am not so naïve as to think that all students will become good as a result of taking religious courses. Clearly, the hoped-for effect would be that a significant number of students develop a growing sense of purpose, so that the predominant atmosphere on campus would change from selfish hedonism to a purposeful community of learners.

A sense of meaninglessness pervades college campuses. To deny it would require us to deny students' destructive behavior, their high attrition, and their incapacity to address society's problems. To address the hedonistic and destructive social habits of college students, to restore in students an informed sense of meaning and purpose for life, and to engage the students in the learning enterprise, colleges must examine the subject of meaning and purpose in the core curriculum.

I can think of no better way to destroy a nation than to corrupt the youth by getting them away from religious faith, by making them superficial and disinterested in governmental and world affairs, and by condoning a world dominated by sex and self-gratification. Engaging in promiscuous sex, excessive drinking, and academic disengagement should be seen as signs of immaturity rather than the college norm. If students are taught that such behavior is self-destructive and inconsonant with their religious beliefs, those students at least are forced to consider their behavior. Such is not the case now.

It is hard to get a perspective on one's own times. But we do know that the cold war dominated much of the last half of the twentieth century, at least until 1987, when the Iron Curtain tumbled. In a similar way, the twentieth century was dominated by an empirical research approach to education. Though there have been obvious benefits, especially technological advancement and material improvement, we are now aware that there are also obvious deficiencies. The richest and most powerful country is in a state of moral and social decay. The country that has stood for goodness and freedom now stands for materialism and promiscuity. Moses said, "You may say to yourself, 'My power and the strength of my hands have produced this wealth for me.' But remember the LORD your God, for it is he who gives you the ability to produce wealth" (Deut. 8:17–18). Jesus said, where your treasure is, there your heart will be also (Matt. 6:21). Aristotle said virtue precedes wealth. De Tocqueville said that if America ceases to be good, America will cease to be great. The saints would all agree: We have sold our soul.

The time has come to admit that students lack meaning and purpose, that helping students become knowledgeable about their religion would be of great service to students, and that such study is an important and appropriate part of a college education.

9

Preparing Your Student to Receive a Good Education

Questions of education start early in life. Do I put my child in day care? In kindergarten? Two or three days a week? What is the school like? Who are the teachers? What are the other kids like? Do I think my child will do well in that environment? These questions continue throughout a child's life, ultimately leading to the question, How do I prepare my child for college and the rest of life?

The Art of Parenting

Any teacher will tell you that parents make a huge difference. The parents who spend time with their kids, helping them read, helping them concentrate, helping them play with others, helping them behave, are the ones whose kids do well in school. One of the saddest comments that I often hear from teachers is "It used to be that when a child got in trouble in school, the child would be in trouble at home. Now when a child gets in trouble in school, the teacher can expect a call from the parents asking what's wrong with the teacher."

When there is a breakdown of the family, the teacher is more important than ever, but the teacher can only do so much. I know a kindergarten teacher in a tough inner-city school who does her best but cannot overcome the lack of support at home. This is why it is often difficult even to get children to learn to read. When schools require parental involvement the results are much better.

By the time your child enters middle school, you need to be thinking about how to prepare the child for college. If the child completes high school without the requisite language and mathematical skills, that child has little chance of succeeding in college. Again, the role of parents or other influential adults is crucial. I know of individuals who, with the right kind of help and encouragement, have passed their GED after only a year or two of study, even after dropping out of school in the eighth grade.

The most important thing that you can do to help your child succeed is to show interest. I don't believe in parents doing homework with children, but I do believe in parents seeing children's homework. Nothing should be of greater concern than children who spend little or no time doing homework in high school. It is hard to expect a child to do well in college if the child cannot do homework in high school.

Another thing you should realize is that no two children can be parented the same way. Some kids need a lot of encouragement. Some need punishment. Some need to learn self-discipline. Some need to be cut off from all electronic input in their lives.

But regardless of differences, parents need to give all children good reasons why they need to apply themselves in school. Bad reasons might be, "You don't want to end up like so-and-so, do you?" Or, "You're just lazy. You won't amount to anything." Or, "Don't you want a good job some day?"

Good reasons are reasons that appeal to children being made in the image of God. There is no telling what a child can accomplish if you believe in that child. Perhaps this is the most important attribute of a parent or teacher—believing in the child and helping the child believe in himself or herself.

There are obstacles in life, certainly. But you should not erect obstacles, nor should you get the child over the obstacles. A parent's role is to *teach* the child how to get over the obstacle. I can remember when my oldest child had a bad elementary schoolteacher. I had to explain to my child that in life he would encounter many such people, bad bosses, bad businessmen, and bad friends. He would have to learn in spite of the fact that he had a bad teacher and realize that although life is not always the way it should be, he should not let that stop him.

Helping Your Child Choose a College

By the time a child enters high school, he or she has developed a vocabulary that probably includes the name of the college or university he or she will attend. The list of college preferences is usually narrowed to a discrete list of colleges by that time. If you think that your child should go somewhere other than the brand-name college with the well-known athletic team, then you should begin to talk about that less well-known college by name.

By the tenth grade, students hear talk in high school about friends going off to college. In the typical high school, the most common names are the local state universities. Tenth graders form impressions and images of what certain schools are like—impressions mostly gained by hearsay from those whom they know, so don't expect the impressions to be very accurate. These impressions probably have more to do with the social aspects of the school than anything else.

Your job is to insert some realism into these impressions and to get the student thinking about why he or she wants to go to college, how much he or she is personally willing to invest in terms of time or money, and what the alternatives might be. As your student begins to think about what he or she would like to get out of college, you need to begin to supply factual information. "This school is very hard to get into. This school has the reputation of being a good learning environment. I know several alumni of this school whom I respect. Why don't you talk to these alumni? If you go to that school, you will need a merit scholarship. You need to begin to think about what you will need to do in high school to get that scholarship."

Though parents often seem reluctant to talk to their children about finances, I think parents should give children a realistic assessment of the likely cost of college. Including tuition and fees, books and supplies, room and board, and transportation and other expenses, the average cost for a student resident in a four-year private college is $27,946 compared to $11,338 for a public college.[1] According to the web site of the National Association of Independent Colleges and Universities (NAICU), the average family income of students in private schools and public schools is about the same. Therefore, if the student attends a private school, he or she needs to get financial aid and may need to earn more money in summer jobs and college work-study programs. The child needs to know that in 1997 the average amount borrowed by 1992–93 graduates was $13,623 for graduates of public four-year institutions and $19,528 for private, non-profit four-year institutions.[2] According to USNews.com, "Most undergraduates misjudge how much they are going to owe and how debt could affect their post-college plans—until senior year, when aid offices provide exit counseling. A recent study for the State Public Interest Research Group found that more than 3 in 4 students underestimate their debt by an average of nearly 5,000, and that many are unfamiliar with their repayment options."[3]

The best decision is one based on the most accurate and pertinent information. The student then needs to consider the evidence in light of his or her personal goals for college. This is the process that you would expect a college graduate to use in solving any problem. However, parents need to understand that most high school students are not accustomed to making such decisions. The process of gathering information, analyzing it, and making decisions is an unfamiliar process for most students. It takes both time and patience on the part of the parent to get the child to focus on something that seems like a long way off.

One way to get students' attention is to have them take the PSAT. The PSAT is taken by all juniors, but sophomores are encouraged to take it as well to get experience. This will give you and the student an indication of how the student is doing in school and how the student does on standardized tests. It will also help you know what to work on and know the range of schools that you can consider in terms of admissions standards.

All college parents know that the high school years are over before you know it, and your most important role might be to keep the student on a timeline that will avoid a last-minute decision based on inadequate information. Students will often balk at such parental involvement, because you will have to push them out of their comfort zone. But this is what you need to do.

Having your student visit colleges with friends is another way to emphasize that the high school experience is rapidly drawing to a close. If you don't have the time or money to do this, you may want to consider getting the church youth director to organize a trip. Or you may trade off with several parents so that you take three or four students at a time but only visit one campus yourself.

The mechanics of choosing a college are less important than developing a rationale for choosing a particular college. As I have already said, the student has to become aware of the importance of his or her own attitude. Getting a student to the point that he or she wants to go to a good college is often the first and hardest step. Don't think that one or two conversations will do it.

Once you think your student is genuinely interested in getting a good education, you need to talk about the importance of the type of students that a school attracts and why. Your child may find it difficult to maintain an interest in getting a good education if few of the other students seem to have that interest. Your child needs to know how many students drop out in the first year.

Finally, you need to help your student look for a learning environment and not just for the glitzy, superficial aspects of a college. Remind your child over and over that college is about two things: teachers and students. Help him or her realize that the college years are most likely the best time in their life to consider what the greatest minds in history said. Help your child understand what it takes to become a professor, learn how to take notes and study for a test, know how to evaluate what the professor says, and know the importance of asking questions and weighing propositions.

College is all about learning to think. Choosing a college is the beginning of the process. And students need to do this, even though they have not been trained to do it. This is why the role of parents and educators is so important. You have to help them know the importance of choosing the right college.

This entire process goes more smoothly if parents help students think of the college choice in light of who they are in the eyes of God. God formed the student before the beginning of time. He put the student in a particular family in a particular city and in a particular era. He created the student to do good works that would bring glory to the Creator. He promised that the student could be an adopted son of God and could call God "Father." God the Father gave his only Son that the student might have abundant life. God the Son promised that his Spirit would enable the student to do far more than the student would ever ask or think possible.

Choosing a college from the perspective of being a child of God changes the whole perspective. A college has the potential to prepare the student to extend God's kingdom into areas of business, government, medicine, or communications in eternally profitable ways. WOW! What an opportunity! Don't miss it.

10

The Lasting Impact of a Life-Changing Education

My favorite question to ask students is, "What are you learning?" The first response usually is, "Do you mean, What am I taking?" I respond by saying, "No, I really want to know what you are learning. What are you learning that affects the way you look at things?"

I am often amazed at what students will tell me. Sometimes they are very open. I am also amazed at where and how they are learning what they are learning. One student told me that he learned more from working for the head groundskeeper than from any professor. Another student told me that she was transformed by her cross-cultural experience. She had had no idea how other people lived. For some students, living with other students, being in accountability groups, and praying together has profoundly affected their self-understanding, especially of their sinful nature and their ability to love others. Many students have told me how much they have learned from a certain professor.

I have come to the conclusion, however, that most students don't begin to appreciate what or how much they learned until about ten years after they have graduated. Many think that they have life all figured out when they graduate; they feel much older and wiser. But ten years later, they have had some hard knocks in their career; they have acquired the responsibilities of a family; they have experienced sickness and death; they have been disappointed by friends; they have experienced marital difficulties; and they know that apart from the grace of God, they can't even love their spouse. Ten years later, those students know they haven't figured out life.

So my favorite question of alumni is, "When you look back on your college experience, what did you really learn?" Two responses emerge. The first thing mentioned is often the depth of friendships. When you think about it, the typical college-bound, middle-class family consists of two children who live in a suburb. Most of these children have never experienced life in a close-knit community. They seldom have neighbors that they know as well as they will come to know friends whom they live with in residence halls. Their parents work, often in organizations with little community.

Then suddenly the students find themselves in a residence hall with two hundred other students, living in a hall with about thirty students. They quickly learn that there are different ideas of noise, musical taste, neatness, consideration, honesty, possessions, studiousness, etc. Covenant College encourages students to become part of a small group of four to eight people. Students use various names for such groups: Bible studies, fellowship groups, prayer groups, accountability groups. We encourage accountability, vulnerability, integrity, dependability, and openness—openness to see yourself as others see you and openness to change. Though everyone does not become part of such a group, the groups have a pervasive influence.

Clearly, alumni cherish the friends they made, often calling them lifelong friends. I suspect that even more than the friendships, they cherish the things they learned from living in such a close-knit community. Being alone in a crowd describes how many people feel unless they have learned what a community is and how to create community wherever one happens to be. And many alumni seemed to learn this in college. Sadly, many college students today do not have such an experience. A parent of a prospective student recently noticed that half the tables in the cafeteria of a large public university were occupied by a person eating alone.

The second thing alumni mention most often is that they learned to think in college. I know many alumni who have demonstrated this in their lives; one who majored in biology and is a banker, one who majored in history and has a Down's syndrome child, one who majored in philosophy and is a small-business owner, one who majored in computer science and lost his sight, and one who went to seminary and decided not to become a minister. When you look at all the twists and turns life takes after college, you realize how important is the ability to think.

I've heard it said that when you study successful people, the only thing they have in common is the ability to rebound from failure. I would say that this shows that they know how to think. One person may be fired and, as a result, develop an image that he or she is incompetent. Another person may be fired and, as a result, decide that he or she needs to change as a person. Learning to think is far more than mere intelligence. None of us uses more than a fraction of our brain. The older I

131

get, the more I realize that for the purpose of analysis, we may divide people up into the emotional, mental, physical, and spiritual aspects of human beings, but the fact is that people are people—affected by a range of internal and external factors.

In so many ways, education is a mystery; we understand so little about the dynamic of a good teacher or a good student. But somehow, the mark of a good education comes down to the ability to think deeply about the purpose and complexity of life. The most difficult thing to think about is God. One reason that the Ten Commandments say that we are not to make an image of God is because the God who created such a universe cannot be put in a box as small as our mind, and we should not try. But when we study God's Word and consider that we are the clay and he is the potter, we are forced to think deeply about life. When students first learn to think about God and then to think about his creation, they know how to think. Only the fool says there is no God.

When you learn to think, you have a treasure that is more valuable than any you could find elsewhere. I'm constantly reminded of a very wealthy person who told me that money has brought her nothing but sadness. I know many people who are successful who just wish they had a friend. Knowing how to think is so much more than being intelligent or successful, and when I probe alumni, I sense that this is what they are saying when they say they learned to think. The mother of the Down's syndrome child has told me that college prepared her to be the mother of the child, and what a wonderful mother she is!

College does not guarantee success, especially if the main thing you received was the ability to say you graduated from a prestigious college. I bought my first pair of shoes from a fifty-year-old graduate of Harvard Business School. I know graduates of all the prestigious schools who have been drunks, deadbeats, broke, divorced, etc. It is an illusion to think that because we went to a certain school, then we will do well. But a college is often where we learn to "frame" what happens to us in life. If our perspective is that life is measured by success, then we all know that only a few are very successful. If our perspective is that life is measured by sex, then we all know that not even half of us find sexual fulfillment. If our perspective is that life is measured by looks, we all know that most of us are pretty ordinary looking. But if our perspective is that we are created in the image of God for his glory, that God is sovereign in all of life, and that he is loving and merciful and forgiving, we have a perspective that works in all circumstances.

I run into people all the time who seemed to learn in college that we evolved as humans and are still in an imperfect state, that the world is in danger of destruction because of our stupidity, that the answer is . . . (you fill in the rest). It is no wonder that for many, life is quiet desperation.

Much of modern academy prides itself on looking at the world objectively. Research, analysis, and reason reign. Others in the academy look at the world bound by culture and the limitations of our personal experience and knowledge. Cultural relativism reigns. Both ways of thinking tend to frame the way we look at the world. But the biblical worldview is still another perspective that is rarely found on campus. The modernist would say that this worldview is based on faith not knowledge. The postmodernist would say that this worldview is just another cultural perspective. Do you want your child to have either perspective?

How do you want your child to view the world after college? Do you think a person can spend four years of study without being affected by the perspective held by his or her esteemed professors? Is college really just about getting a good job? Should it be?

How will you talk to your student about the lasting impact of a life-changing education?

Notes

Introduction

1. "The Nation," *The Chronicle of Higher Education, Almanac Issue* (31 August 2001): 7. *The Chronicle of Higher Education* is the trade journal of education and did not come into existence until 1967. It was not until 1989 that *The Chronicle* began to publish its "Almanac Issue," an annual issue that gives a statistical overview of higher education. The development of *The Chronicle* is further evidence of the growth and maturation of higher education.

Chapter 1: *What Do You Want from Your Child's Education?*

1. U.S. Census Bureau, "Statistical Abstract of the U.S.: 2000," 470.

Chapter 2: *College Education Today*

1. *AAC&U Peer Review, Association of American Colleges and Universities* (fall 1998): 3.

2. Ibid., 3.

3. "Integrity in the College Curriculum: A Report to the Academic Community," Association of American Colleges, 1985, 3–4.

4. "Statistical Abstract of the U.S.: 2000," U.S. Census Bureau, 127.

5. "College Enrollment by Age of Students," *The Chronicle of Higher Education, Almanac Issue* (31 August 2001): 20.

6. All data is from the *Digest of Educational Statistics*, U.S. Center for Education Statistics, except for the 1995 figures, which are from *The Chronicle of Higher Education, Almanac Issue*, 5.

7. "Integrity in the College Curriculum: A Report to the Academic Community," 4.

8. Ibid., 3–4.

9. David W. Breneman, *Liberal Arts Colleges* (Washington, D.C.: Brookings Institution, 1994), 139.

10. "The Dissolution of General Education: 1914–1993," *The National Association of Scholars*, 2.

11. Ibid., 6.

12. "Yale Relies on TAs and Adjuncts for Teaching, Report Says," *The Chronicle of Higher Education* (9 April 1999): A15. A study by graduate students at Yale found that tenured and tenure-track faculty members are responsible for only 30 percent of undergraduate classroom instruction, while graduate students and adjunct instructors together handle 70 percent of undergraduate teaching.

13. "The Knowledge Factory," *The Economist* (4 October 1997): 3.

Chapter 3: *Understanding Teens*

1. *The Encyclopedia Britannica*, Fourth Edition, vol. 18 (New York: Encyclopedia Britannica, Inc., 1929), 233.

2. George Gallup and Jim Castelli, *People's Religion: American Faith in the 90's* (New York: Macmillan, 1989).

3. Ibid., 60.

Chapter 4: *Helping Students Ask the Right Questions*

1. "Improving the College Experience," National Survey of Student Enjoyment (Bloomington, Ind.: Indiana University Center for Post Secondary Research and Planning), 11.

2. Some of the questions highlighted in the November 17, 2000, issue are as follows:

1. Campus environment emphasizes spending significant amounts of time studying and on academic work.
   a. Very little (3.1% of seniors)
   b. Some (18.2% of seniors)
   c. Quite a bit (41.9% of seniors)
   d. Very much (36.8% of seniors)
2. Number of written papers or reports of 20 pages or more.
   a. None (47.2% of seniors)
   b. Fewer than 5 (42.7% of seniors)
   c. Between 5 and 10 (7.4% of seniors)
   d. Between 11 and 20 (1.8% of seniors)
   e. More than 20 (1.0% of seniors)

3. Number of hours per week spent preparing for class (studying, reading, writing, rehearsing, and other activities related to your academic program).
4. Discussed ideas from your reading or classes with faculty members outside of class.
5. Worked with faculty members on activities other than course work (committees, orientation, student life activities, etc.).
6. Had serious conversations with students with religious beliefs, political opinions, or personal values very different from yours.
7. Had serious conversations with students of a different race or ethnicity than your own.

3. "Are Students Actually Learning?" *The Chronicle of Higher Education* (17 November 2000): A71.

4. Breneman, *Liberal Arts Colleges,* 141, from Eric L. Dey, Alexander W. Astin, and William S. Korn, *The American Freshman: Twenty-Five Year Trends, 1966–1990* (Los Angeles: Higher Education Research Institute, UCLA, 1991).

5. L. J. Sax, Alexander W. Astin, William S. Korn, K. M. Mahoney, *The American Freshman: National Norms for Fall 1996* (Los Angeles: Higher Education Research Institute, UCLA, 1996), 15.

6. Kenneth L. Woodward, "Young beyond Their Years," *Newsweek* (Special Issue, winter 1989/spring 1990): 54–55.

7. Arthur Levine and Jeanette S. Cureton, "College Life, an Obituary," *Change* (May/June 1998): 14.

8. *The Chronicle of Higher Education, Almanac Issue* (31 August 2001): 18.

9. In this section, I have not delved into the issue of the culture of community colleges or commuter colleges.

Chapter 6: *What Students Need from a College Education*

1. I give credit for these thoughts to Ernest Boyer, the former head of the Carnegie Foundation, from a talk he gave at the annual meeting of the Southern Association of Colleges and Schools.

2. Dr. Richard Paul and Dr. Linda Edder, *The Miniature Guide to Critical Thinking,* The Foundation for Critical Thinking (www.criticalthinking.org).

3. Ernest T. Pascarella and Patrick T. Terenzini, *How College Affects Students* (San Francisco: Jossey-Bass, 1991).

Chapter 7: *Why Colleges Fail to Give Students What They Need*

1. To gain further insight into the problems of this, I highly recommend reading George Marsden, *The Outrageous Idea of Christian Scholarship* (New York: Oxford University Press, 1997).

Chapter 8: *A Curriculum That Develops Knowledgeable Faith*

1. Robert Wuthnow, *The Restructuring of American Religion* (Princeton: Princeton University Press, 1988), 156–58, 161.

2. George Marsden, *The Soul of the American University* (New York: Oxford University Press, 1994).

3. "Tracking America's Soul," *Christianity Today* (17 November 1989): 23–24.

Chapter 9: *Preparing Your Student to Receive a Good Education*

1. "Average College Costs 2000–2001," *The Chronicle of Higher Education, Almanac Issue* (31 August 2001): 33.

2. "Statistical Abstract of the U.S.: 2001," U.S. Census Bureau, 172.

3. www.usnews.com (13 December 2001).

Recommended Books
for Further Reading

AAUP Policy Documents & Reports. Washington, D.C., 1990.

Astin, Alexander W. *Four Critical Years.* San Francisco: Jossey-Bass, 1977.

———. *What Matters in College?* San Francisco: Jossey-Bass, 1993.

Boyer, Ernest L. *Scholarship Reconsidered, Priorities of the Professoriate.* New Jersey: The Carnegie Foundation for the Advancement of Teaching, 1990.

———. *The Control of the Campus.* Washington, D.C.: The Carnegie Foundation for the Advancement of Teaching, 1982.

Gallup, George and Jim Castelli. *People's Religion: American Faith in the 90's.* New York: Macmillan, 1989.

Lessons Learned from FIPSE Projects II. United States Department of Education, 1993.

Marsden, George M. *The Soul of the American University.* New York: Oxford University Press, 1994.

Neuhaus, Richard John. *The Naked Public Square.* Grand Rapids: Wm. B. Eerdmans, 1984.

Palmer, Parker J. *The Courage to Teach.* San Francisco: Jossey-Bass, 1998.

Pascarella, Ernest T., and Patrick T. Terenzini. *How College Affects Students.* San Francisco: Jossey-Bass, 1991.

Willimon, William H., and Thomas H. Naylor. *The Abandoned Generation.* Grand Rapids: Wm. B. Eerdmans, 1995.

Wingspread Group on Higher Education. *An American Imperative.* The Johnson Foundation, 1993.

Wuthnow, Robert. *The Restructuring of American Religion.* Princeton: Princeton University Press, 1988.